BRF Newsletter

At the time of writing (July 1992) it seems remarkable that it is only one year since BRF's headquarters moved out of London to our new home here in Oxford. It has been a time with much to do: with new team members—Karen, Chris and Leanne—settling into their roles, with new computer systems, and with new editors for *Guidelines* and *First Light* (as the former editors, John Rogerson, Chris Rowland and Jan Ainsworth handed over to their successors).

It has been a time to look back—to think of all those who have gone before us in BRF over the past seventy years and to thank God for their vision and for all the hard work which has gone into making BRF what it is now. It is also a time to look forward—to the opportunities and challenges which lie before us. We are excited about what God has in store for BRF.

It seems rather strange to be writing the BRF Newsletter nearly nine months before you will come to read it, and yet we have to do this. We need to print the notes and have them delivered back to us in time to be able to send them out all over the world (are you aware that the notes are read in 62 countries worldwide?) so that our readers receive them in good time before the start of the issue. In one sense the news I am writing now will be old news when you read it at the beginning of May 1993, yet we want to keep you in touch through the notes with what is happening in BRF, even if you will read about it long after the event.

Over the past year it has been exciting to see the developments in the notes. Certainly your letters, for which we are always grateful, suggest that you too are pleased with what you are finding in *New Daylight* and *Guidelines*. We have seen an increasing amount of devotional material in *Guidelines* (this had been requested by many readers). The response to the new large print version of *New Daylight* has been very positive. And now we also have the special one month sample edition of *New Daylight*, which offers a taste of the notes from the regular writing team . . . an ideal way of introducing someone to *New Daylight* for the first time.

It's always good to be able to tell you of new BRF publications which may be of interest to you. By the time you read this the books mentioned below will all be available.

Many of you will know of Michael Marshall—former Bishop of Woolwich, Director of the Anglican Institute, and regular back page columnist of *The Church of England Newspaper*. Michael Marshall wrote *Just Like Him*, BRF's Lent Book for 1989, and *Great Expectations?* in 1991, a group study book for evangelism in parishes. This summer (1992) he returned to the UK to head, jointly with Canon Michael Green, *Springboard*, the Archbishops' (of Canterbury and York) new initiative for the Decade of Evangelism. Both Michael Marshall and Michael Green will be travelling widely throughout the UK, speaking and preaching, as they lead this new venture.

Michael Marshall's book *Great Expectations?* has sold out, and so to mark the author's return to the UK, we have published a new edition, with a new, expanded introduction, and with a new title: *Expectations for Evangelism—a user-friendly guide to parish based evangelism* (price £4.99). The book contains a six-week Bible study course on parish evangelism based on the Acts of the Apostles.

Another new publication is a fully revised edition of *Our World, God's World* (price £3.99) by Barbara Wood, the daughter of E. F. Schumacher. Originally published for Advent, *Our World, God's World* has been largely re-written, and has been updated and expanded. Six weeks of material that is relevant for use at any time of the year, it explores how we as Christians have a responsibility to share God's love for the world around us—the world that he created and still creates. Group study and worship material is also included.

And finally four exciting new titles which together provide a simple step-by-step Bible study programme which begins at the beginning and aims to put the Bible into the hands of ordinary people. The four titles (price £2.99 each) are *Step by Step to Knowing God* (Volume 1), *Step by Step with Jesus* (Volume 2), *Step by Step to the Coming King* (Volume 3) and *Step by Step with the*

Growing Church (Volume 4). Each book is divided into twelve studies and each study into six daily sections. There is an introductory statement for each study and then a series of readings and questions for each day. Volumes 1 and 2 will be available from January 1993 and we expect Volumes 3 and 4 to be available from the end of April.

And so, as we come to send these notes off to be printed (in Denmark), we give thanks for every one of you our readers and supporters and we pray that each of us, through our prayer and Bible reading, may come to a deeper knowledge and love of God and of his son, Jesus Christ.

With every good wish

Richard Fisher

General Manager

From the Editor

This morning I had a letter from a reader of *New Daylight* with a PS which was a very mild complaint. 'Pentecost means very little!' she wrote. 'The Greek means fiftieth day.' And she went on to say, 'Trinity reinforces the three-foldness of Father, Son and Holy Ghost—much more comforting surely?' Ever since I read them I have been thinking about those two comments, because they are both relevant to the Church today—and to this issue of *New Daylight*, which includes Pentecost and Trinity Sunday and also the teaching which Jesus gave to his disciples about the Holy Spirit before he died.

'Pentecost means very little,' my correspondent wrote—and it is a sad fact that what she says is true for far too many Christians. They know that the book of Acts tells of astonishing events that took place on the Day of Pentecost. But that was two thousand years ago, and there doesn't seem to be much connection between what happened then and their present experience.

Yet other Christians, in the traditional churches as well as the Pentecostal Church, have discovered to their delight that there is a connection—and as a result their Christian lives have been touched by the Holy Spirit of God and grown fresh and green like parched grass after rain.

Pentecost does mean 'the fiftieth day'. The astonishing events took place on the old Jewish festival of firstfruits, celebrated at the start of the wheat harvest, on the fiftieth day after the Feast of Passover. At that feast they would have eaten a lamb, roasted with bitter herbs, to remember the Exodus of the Jews from Egypt, and to remember that when the blood of the lamb was put on the doorposts and lintel of their houses the angel of death would 'pass over' them and they would live (Exodus 12:1–14).

The New Testament writers say that Christ shed his blood 'for us'. They write of those who have 'washed their robes, and made them white in the blood of the Lamb' (Revelation 7:14). They report that John the Baptist pointed to Jesus and said, 'Look, the Lamb of God, who takes away the sin of the world!'; and also said that he is the one 'who will baptize with the Holy Spirit . . . ' (John 1:29,33).

Christ was crucified at the Passover, and on the fiftieth day after that the Spirit came—on the festival at the beginning of the wheat harvest. Jesus had said, 'Unless a grain of wheat falls into the earth and dies, it remains alone; but if it dies, it bears much fruit . . . ' Jesus had died—and now at the festival of firstfruits the grain of wheat was bearing much fruit. Three thousand Christian converts after Peter's preaching on the Day of Pentecost—the fiftieth day after the death of Christ, and the birthday of the Christian Church.

It wasn't until the fourth century that they started to talk about God as Trinity. We shall be looking at that on Trinity Sunday, and at the wonder of the nature of the Godhead—Father, Son and Holy Spirit—in the first two weeks of May. That is in my notes on John 13 and 14 in our series *Great Chapters of the Bible*. Many Christians today *don't* find the doctrine of the Trinity comforting, because they find it difficult to understand. But we shall discover the comfort and the glory of it through our hearts and not our heads, and through praying and experience rather than thinking.

Then Douglas Cleverley Ford will help us to worship God through the Psalms, which were the prayerbook of the Old Testament. The disciples would have prayed the Psalms in the synagogue (and in the upper room) while they waited for the promise of the Spirit after the Ascension of Jesus. We shall look at the Ascension, and at the plans the disciples made to fill the place of Judas. Then we shall go on praying the Psalms until the day of Pentecost. Rosemary Green takes us through the first few chapters of Acts and helps us to connect what happened then with what can happen (and in some places is happening) now.

After the exhilaration of Pentecost we go back with Marcus Maxwell to the life of Elijah, who prophesied in the power of the Holy Spirit. We say in the Creeds that God 'spoke through the prophets', and after we have heard the Word of God through Elijah we look at the Word of God in the Old and the New Testaments. A new writer in the *New Daylight* team helps us to do that, Dom Henry Wansbrough. He is superbly qualified to do so, as a scholar and the General Editor of the New Jerusalem Bible.

In the first half of August we go to Joyce Huggett's *School of Prayer* (Part 2), and she helps us to deepen our prayer life and to know God better in the process. In the second half we discover *Reality and Truth and God* with Adrian Plass. Through some Bible passages that have meant a lot to Adrian, and through his comments, we find out in a fresh way how the truth can set us free. It happens through Jesus—the Way, the Truth and the Life.

We still pray here in Oxford just before nine o'clock every morning, for you, for ourselves, and for the worldwide ministry of the BRF. We know that some of you join us then—and Richard Fisher, Karen Teal, Leanne Little, Chris Samways and I send you our greetings and our love.

Shelagh Brown

Editor

The Bible Reading Fellowship Prayer

We bless you, Lord,
For all who teach us
To love the Scriptures
And for all who help us
To understand them;
Grant that in
The written Word
We may encounter
The living Word
Your Son, our Saviour,
Jesus Christ.
Amen.

Norman Wallwork

SPREAD THE WORD

Why not help us to spread the word about the Fellowship by
giving a Gift Subscription to a friend or a member of your family?
To do this, just fill in the coupon below and send it to:

The Bible Reading Fellowship
Peter's Way
Sandy Lane West
Oxford OX4 5HG

Name of person to receive the Gift Subscription:

_____

Address_____

_____

_____Postcode_____

Please send to the above, beginning with the May/Sept 1993 issue
(delete as appropriate)

FIRST LIGHT	☐	7.95
GUIDELINES	☐	7.95
NEW DAYLIGHT	☐	7.95
NEW DAYLIGHT LARGE PRINT	☐	12.00

(Please tick box)
I enclose cheque/postal order for _____ made out to BRF.

Your Name_____

Your Address_____

_____

_____Postcode_____

ORDER FORM

Please send me the following book(s):

	Quantity	Unit Price	Total
Expectations for Evangelism	_____	4.99	_____
Our World, God's World	_____	3.99	_____
Step by Step to Knowing God	_____	2.99	_____
Step by Step with Jesus	_____	2.99	_____
Step by Step to the Coming King	_____	2.99	_____
Step by Step with the Growing Church	_____	2.99	_____

Total Cost of Books _____

Add 15% to cover postage & packing (min. 85p) _____
(Orders over £25 will be sent post free) _____

TOTAL _____

I enclose a cheque/postal order payable to: The Bible Reading Fellowship for the sum of _____
Please send my order to:

Name_____

Address_____

_____

_____Postcode_____

BRF Account Number (if applicable) _____

Send this completed Order Form, with your remittance to:
The Bible Reading Fellowship
Peter's Way, Sandy Lane West
Oxford OX4 5HG

God with us—the Holy Spirit

In the months before my father died he started to talk to me about his impending death. I don't know how he knew about it. Perhaps a combination of worsening angina and an intuitive sense of what lay ahead. But I didn't want to hear what he was saying—any more than the disciples of Jesus wanted to hear what he was saying.

In chapters 12 to 17 of John's Gospel Jesus is telling his disciples what is going to happen. But they don't understand and they are deeply upset. When we love someone we don't want them to go away and leave us in the separation of death, even though as Christians we know that isn't the end of the story.

'I don't want to leave you,' my father said to me, 'but I know that I'll see you again.' It was the day before he died and his premonition had been right. A severe pain in his chest woke him up in the middle of the night and it wasn't indigestion (as I desperately hoped) but a heart attack. He was facing his death with a lot of faith and only a little fear. He had become a Christian at the age of sixty-five, and now he had just reached his three-score years and ten.

In those five intervening years his faith had grown from an acorn into a sturdy oak tree. He believed that Jesus had forgiven all his sins (and there were plenty of them!). He also believed that because of Jesus' resurrection there would be a resurrection for him as well. That was when he would see me again—together with my mother, and all those who had 'died in faith'. It made all the difference in the world to dying.

But the disciples didn't know all that. Not then. Not until after the first Easter morning. Then they knew that Jesus was alive—and they went all over the known world preaching 'Jesus and resurrection'.

Then the four Gospel writers put the message on papyrus, and Luke extended his Gospel into the Acts of the Apostles. But those acts were really the acts of the Holy Spirit of Jesus. That was what Jesus had been telling them about in the days before he died.

'Because I have said these things, you are filled with grief. But I tell you the truth: it is for your good that I am going away. Unless I go away, the Counsellor will not come to you; but if I go, I will send him to you' (John 16:6,7).

We cannot study now all the great chapters in John about God's future plans for the lovers and followers of Jesus, but in future issues of *New Daylight* we will. Now we shall look at the end of chapter 13 and the whole of chapter 14.

Shelagh Brown

Prayers for the Decade of Evangelism in the season of Pentecost

Lord of Light—shine on us,
Lord of Peace—dwell in us,
Lord of Might—succour us,
Lord of Love—enfold us,
Lord of Wisdom—enlighten us.

Then Lord, let us go out as your witnesses, in obedience to your command,
to share the Good News of your love for us in the gift of your Son, our Saviour, Jesus Christ.

St Asaph: Mothers' Union (Wales)

Almighty God, we thank you for having renewed your Church, at various times and in various ways, by rekindling the fire of love for you through the work of your Holy Spirit. Rekindle your love in our hearts and renew us to fulfil the Great Commission which your Son committed to us; so that, individually and collectively, as members of your Church, we may help many to know Jesus Christ as their Lord and Saviour. Empower us by your Spirit to share, with our neighbours and friends, our human stories in the context of your divine story; through Jesus Christ our Lord. Amen.

West Malaysia

We acknowledge these prayers with thanks to the Decade of Evangelism, The Anglican Communion, Partnership House, 157 Waterloo Road, London SE1 8UT.

John 13:31–33 (NIV)

Going away

When he was gone, Jesus said, 'Now is the Son of Man glorified and God is glorified in him. If God is glorified in him, God will glorify the Son in himself, and will glorify him at once. My children, I will be with you only a little longer. You will look for me, and just as I told the Jews, so I tell you now: Where I am going, you cannot come.'

It was Judas who had gone—to betray Jesus. John says that 'he went out. And it was night.' Judas had gone out from the presence of the light of the world into the darkness. Now Jesus would tell the disciples who were left what lay ahead, for him and for them.

Hundreds of years before the birth (and the death) of Christ, Isaiah had written down words of prophecy about a suffering servant: 'And now the Lord says—he who formed me in the womb to be his servant... "It is too small a thing for you to be my servant to restore the tribes of Jacob... I will also make you a light for the Gentiles, that you may bring my salvation to the ends of the earth"' (Isaiah 49:5,6).

Jesus had taken that prophecy and applied it to himself: 'I am the light of the world: he who follows me shall not walk in darkness but shall have the light of life.' They would have it because on the cross the light of the world would go into the darkness and desolation of sin—for their sake, and because he loved them. Then everyone in the world would know just how much God loved the world (and every individual in it). They would know what God was really like, as the glory of God shone out brighter than the sun from the cross of Christ. But first he had to die—and the disciples would only have his physical presence with them for a little longer.

A reflection

What would you have felt like if you had been there when Jesus said he was going away? What do you feel like when you face a future of change and separation? Can you manage to say 'Peace, perfect peace, our future all unknown. Jesus we know, and he is on the throne?'

Bishop Bickersteth

Isaiah 61:1,2a (NIV)

Through prayer and the Spirit

The Gospel of Luke says that when Jesus began his ministry he was about thirty years old. But before he began he was baptised by John in the River Jordan, and 'as he was praying, heaven was opened and the Holy Spirit descended on him in bodily form like a dove. And a voice came from heaven: "You are my Son, whom I love; with you I am well pleased"' (Luke 3:22).

But then something strange happened. Jesus came back from the Jordan 'full of the Holy Spirit', and was led by the Spirit into the desert, 'where for forty days he was tempted by the devil'. Oscar Wilde wrote that 'The only way to get rid of a temptation is to yield to it.' But Jesus never yielded to it. He fought off the tempter every time with the word of God, which is the sword of the Spirit: 'Scripture says... scripture says... scripture says...'

After the temptation Jesus returned to Galilee 'in the power of the Spirit, and news about him spread through the whole countryside' (Luke 4:14). Then he went to his home town, Nazareth, and on the Sabbath he went to the synagogue and read aloud from the prophet Isaiah.

The Spirit of the Sovereign Lord is on me, because the Lord has anointed me to preach good news to the poor. He has sent me to bind up the broken-hearted, to proclaim freedom for the captives and release from darkness for the prisoners, to proclaim the year of the Lord's favour.

Everything happened through the power of the Spirit. The birth of Jesus. The baptism of Jesus. The leading into the desert to be tested by temptation, and the successful resistance of Jesus. Then the ministry of Jesus. That is how it happened for Jesus and that is how it will happen for us. When the Spirit indwells a human being (and Jesus *was* a human being) God and man are in union and communion. Total union and unbroken communion for the Father and the Son. Imperfect union and communion for the Father and the 'sons and daughters of God'. But the same sort of indwelling—and the same sort of temptations—and the same sort of work to be done. Through the power of the Spirit, and through the prayer that keeps us connected to the God of love.

John 13:34,35 (NIV)

Love like Jesus

'A new command I give you: Love one another. As I have loved you, so you must love one another. By this all men will know that you are my disciples, if you love one another.'

Jesus wasn't saying anything new when he told them to love one another. Other rabbis had said the same, and it was there at the heart of the holiness code back in Leviticus. 'You shall love your neighbour as yourself' (19:18), it said, in a set of instructions for the priests and the people about how to live the whole of their life in a holy way that was pleasing to God. But Jesus had gone much further than that. His followers were to love their enemies as well as their friends, and that was to love 'As I have loved you . . . ' Paul—once the enemy of Jesus—had discovered the wonder of that sort of loving, and seen it in the death of Christ:

But God demonstrates his own love for us in this: While we were still sinners, Christ died for us. Since we have now been justified by his blood, how much more shall we be saved from God's wrath through him! For if, when we were God's enemies, we were reconciled to him through the death of his Son, how much more, having been reconciled, shall we be saved through his life!

(Romans 5:8–10)

A reflection

'See how these Christians love one another!' someone said about those early Christians. Ask yourself if they would say it about you, and about your church. Then ask God if he would say it about you, and about your church. 'As I have loved you, so you must love one another.' If you don't love like that confess it, repent, and pray for the gift of the Holy Spirit to help you to love like Jesus.

John 13:36–38 (NIV)

You are . . . you will be

Simon Peter asked him, 'Lord, where are you going?' Jesus replied, 'Where I am going, you cannot follow now, but you will follow later.' Peter asked, 'Lord, why can't I follow you now? I will lay down my life for you.' Then Jesus answered, 'Will you really lay down your life for me? I tell you the truth, before the cock crows, you will disown me three times!'

A small girl I know isn't very good at knowing her own limitations. She loves her food, and when she sees one of her favourite dishes on the table she demands a big helping. One day when she had come to lunch her face gleamed with pleasure at the prospect of roast lamb, roast potatoes and peas. But when she saw the size of the helping I had put on her plate she scowled. 'More!', she said. 'No,' I said, 'You won't finish it. You can have some more when you've finished this.' 'No—now!' she said, getting cross. So I gave her what she insisted she could eat, and warned her that if she didn't finish it she wouldn't have any ice-cream and butterscotch sauce afterwards. Afterwards arrived, and we sat there for a long time while other people ate their ice-cream and she refused to eat the rest of her roast potatoes. It had a fairly happy ending—with concessions made on both sides.

Like Peter, my young friend didn't know herself very well. Peter thought he could manage more than he could for the sake of Jesus. But Jesus knew just what Peter could and couldn't manage. 'You are Simon . . . ' Jesus said, 'You will be called Cephas' (which means rock). Dr Campbell Morgan says that Jesus knows what he can do with Peter. He can take the little rock that he is—the shifting, shaley sand of human nature—and transform it into Petros, the divine nature. Perhaps there is an echo of that in 2 Peter 1:3,4: 'His divine power has given us everything that we need . . . He has given us his very great and precious promises, so that through them you may participate in the divine nature . . . '

A prayer
Lord Jesus, help me to know my limitations, and also to know you. By your divine power (and because you love me) may I share your divine nature. Amen.

John 14:1-3 (NIV)

A place for me

'Do not let your hearts be troubled. Trust in God; trust also in me. In my Father's house are many rooms; if it were not so, I would have told you. I am going there to prepare a place for you. And if I go and prepare a place for you, I will come back and take you to be with me that you also may be where I am.'

The disciples know now that Jesus is going away—and he knows that they are troubled. So he speaks to them to comfort them—and what he said to them still comforts people and is often read out at funerals. A Christian man who hadn't very long to live told me once how much he loved this passage.

'I look on it rather like this. When I was a boy we came back from New Zealand. I was aged about twelve and my father was looking for a parish. I went straight to a preparatory school and during my first term there he was appointed to a parish in Buckinghamshire. At the end of the term I travelled by train to his new parish—and when I got out at the station there he was to meet me . . . and to drive me home. And the home he took me to I had never seen before, but when I got there I was shown up to a room and there were some of my familiar things around me. My father and my mother were there—and that was home. There wasn't a great problem about adjusting at all—and I rather feel that heaven is going to be like that. First of all we shall have our Father and the Lord Jesus Christ there, and that in some way it will probably be not as unfamiliar as we think. But he will have prepared a place for us and we will know it—as our place.' (*Drawing Near to the City, Christians speak about dying*, Shelagh Brown)

A prayer

Lord Jesus, thank you that you have gone to prepare a place for us— and that means a place for me. Thank you that one day you will come and take me there—and that I'll be with you for ever. I shall like that—and I'm looking forward to it. But I'm still a bit frightened of dying. Help me not to be— whenever it happens. Amen.

John 14:4–6 (NIV)

How can we know?

[Jesus said] 'You know the way to the place where I am going.' Thomas said to him, 'Lord, we don't know where you are going, so how can we know the way?' Jesus answered, 'I am the way and the truth and the life. No one comes to the Father except through me.'

I love the way that Thomas is brave enough to contradict Jesus. 'You know the way to the place where I am going,' says Jesus, and Thomas immediately says, 'How can we? We don't know *where* you are going!' It's a valid point. But if Thomas had really been listening to what Jesus had just been saying, then he would have known. Jesus is going to his Father's house. There are many rooms there (and one of them would be Thomas' room—a place for Thomas). The way into the Father's house is through the Son—and earlier on in John's Gospel Jesus has used the picture of a sheep-fold and a shepherd: 'I tell you the truth, I am the gate for the sheep... whoever enters through me will be saved. He will come in and go out, and find pasture... I have come that they may have life, and have it to the full. I am the good shepherd. The good shepherd lays down his life for the sheep' (John 10:7,9,11).

The Son who is the good shepherd will give his life for the sheep. But he isn't a dead shepherd or a dead son. He's alive! (They don't know that yet, but they will.) God the Son is the true (not false) and living (not dead) way to God the Father. Perhaps we don't have to 'be a Christian' to come to God. But whoever comes must know something of the true nature of God—that she or he comes to a God who is loving, merciful and forgiving. No one can thrust into the holy presence of God holding out the entry ticket of their own good life. Merit won't get anyone in. But I believe that the mercy of God will let anyone in who asks for that mercy.

A prayer

Lord Jesus, help me to listen to you—and to ask you questions (like Thomas) when I don't understand (and when perhaps I haven't listened). Thank you that you are the way, the truth and the life—and that you are merciful.
Amen.

John 14:7–9 (NIV)

Seeing God

Now it is Philip who isn't understanding Jesus. Philip has been listening, but what Jesus has said is mind-blowing:

'If you really knew me, you would know my Father as well. From now on, you do know him and have seen him.'

What a thing for a Jew to say! That really to know him is also to know God the Father. And not just to *know* God the Father but to have *seen* him as well. How can they have seen him? But they want to.

Philip said, 'Lord, show us the Father and that will be enough for us.' Jesus answered: 'Don't you know me, Philip, even after I have been among you such a long time? Anyone who has seen me has seen the Father. How can you say, "Show us the Father"?'

Some rather silly Christians say that we cannot say anything about God, since God is beyond all our understanding and imagining and words cannot describe him. But the Son whom John says is the Word of God had no such hang-ups.

Anyone who has seen me has seen the Father.

Bishop John Robinson once wrote that in Jesus we can see 'the human face of God'. To know what Jesus is like is to know what God is like. So God sits down at a table and has a party with sinners—and he invites them to a party that is also a wedding. The wedding of his Son to his bride the Church, and the Church is made up of beloved and forgiven sinners. The Son who is also the Shepherd gave his life for them—and the Shepherd is also 'The Lamb of God, who takes away the sin of the world' (John 1:29). One image isn't enough to tell us what God is like. But the one and only Son can tell us—and show us. 'No one has ever seen God; the only Son, who is in the bosom of the Father, he has made him known' (John 1:18 RSV).

A prayer

Father God, I am so glad that you are like Jesus. Jesus, thank you so much for showing us what your Father is like. Amen.

19

John 14:10,11 (NIV)

Believe me!

'Don't you believe that I am in the Father, and that the Father is in me? The words I say to you are not just my own. Rather, it is the Father, living in me, who is doing his work. Believe me when I say that I am in the Father and the Father is in me; or at least believe on the evidence of the miracles themselves.'

Jesus is saying a terrible thing. Terrible if it isn't true and terrible if it is. Terrible meaning 'extremely bad' if he is making a false claim about himself. Terrible with the meaning 'awesome' if what he claims is true. But I have never heard anyone say that Jesus was 'bad'. Muslims, who believe that 'there is one God, Allah', put Jesus among their prophets (though lower down than Muhammad). They say we have got our belief about Jesus wrong because our Scriptures are corrupted. But those who know about these things say that they are probably the best attested documents in history. It is unreasonable to say that Jesus was a good man who gave us the greatest moral teaching the world has ever known. The Gospel writers don't leave us that option.

We don't have to be able to explain it. We just have to put our trust in Jesus and follow him. We can study his life in the Gospels and reflect on it in the rest of the New Testament. And we shall understand the New even better if we study the Old. It was Jesus' 'Bible', and, as we read last Sunday, Luke says that at the start of his ministry he read it out in the synagogue: 'The Spirit of the Lord is on me, because he has anointed me to preach good news to the poor . . .' (Luke 4:18).

A reflection

Read again the words from John and from Luke. In silence, let them sink into you. Let them stay inside you—and deepen your faith in Jesus, the Christ (or anointed one) of God and the Son of God.

Listen to me

Those whom I love I rebuke and discipline. So be earnest and repent. Here I am! I stand at the door and knock. If anyone hears my voice and opens the door, I will come in and eat with him, and he with me. To him who overcomes, I will give the right to sit with me on my throne, just as I overcame and sat down with my Father on his throne. He who has an ear, let him hear what the Spirit says to the churches.

On Sundays in New Daylight we almost always reflect on Holy Communion or on prayer, and today we shall think about prayer as listening. It is the Son of God who is speaking to John in a shining and brilliant vision of himself on the Island of Patmos: 'Do not be afraid. I am the First and the Last. I am the Living One; I was dead and behold I am alive for ever and ever!' The risen Christ stands among the churches and tells them to listen. Not just the churches of that day. The churches now. And if we are Christians we are all members of a local church as well as the one Church of Christ. The glorious, risen Christ, with his eyes blazing like fire, who sees all the things that we do and knows all that we fail to do, is knocking at our door wanting to come in. He won't force his way into a church, any more than he will force his way into a human heart. This verse is often used when a person wants to become a Christian and invite Christ into his or her life, and I prayed it myself when I invited him into mine. But we aren't just individuals with Christ living in us. We are the body of Christ—and at Holy Communion today we shall say that we are. Christ wants to come into our church—and to sit down at table and eat with us as he did with the sinners in Galilee two thousand years ago.

Perhaps the body of Christ in our church needs to get on its knees and listen in silence and to hear what the Spirit says to our church. Dare we do it? Christ tells us to, because he loves us. He also loves the world so much that he died for it. And half of the world is hungry, and some of the people in it are homeless. Many people are sick—and most people are sad. So what is the Spirit saying to the churches?

SB

John 14:12–14 (NIV)

Have faith in me

'I tell you the truth, anyone who has faith in me will do what I have been doing. He will do even greater things than these, because I am going to the Father. And I will do whatever you ask in my name, so that the Son may bring glory to the Father. You may ask me for anything in my name, and I will do it.'

Some people find these words very hard to believe—and they think wistfully, 'If only I had more faith then I would be able to heal the sick and feed the hungry and perform miracles. Whatever I prayed for would happen—if only I had more faith...' And the person feels depressed and a bit feeble. Yet if we add up how many hospitals have been founded and run in the name of Christ, and how many hungry have been fed by Christian organizations, then Christians have done 'more' healings, and fed 'more' people than Jesus did on earth.

We tend to hanker after miracles. And sometimes they happen. But it doesn't seem to be the norm. In yesterday's passage Jesus asks his disciples to believe what he says about his relationship with the Father. But if they can't manage to believe just because of his words then perhaps they can believe on the evidence of the miracles. It's rather like Thomas' encounter with the risen Christ: 'Unless I see the nail marks in his hands and put my finger where the nails were, and put my hand into his side, I will not believe,' he says to the other disciples. A week later Jesus comes and stands among the disciples and invites Thomas to do what he wanted. It doesn't say whether Thomas does it or not. Simply that 'Thomas said to him, "My Lord and my God!" Then Jesus told him, "Because you have seen me you have believed; blessed are those who have not seen and yet have believed"' (John 20:28–29).

A reflection

Jesus says he will do anything that we ask in his name. The key to unlocking that is always to pray 'Your will be done'. Then it will be—though if we pray it for someone else they can resist and refuse both the love and the will of God. 'Do you want to get well?' Jesus asks (John 5:6). What if the answer is 'No'?

John 14:15–17 (NIV)

Obey me and love me

'If you love me, you will obey what I command. And I will ask the Father, and he will give you another Counsellor to be with you for ever—the Spirit of truth. The world cannot accept him, because it neither sees him nor knows him. But you know him, for he lives with you and will be in you.'

It seems strange to link love with obedience. But in our own culture it happens all the time—though not in the way that Jesus meant it. For us love is about lovely feelings and freedom—and love can be a total dictator. If two people fall in love then love says to them 'You must follow your hearts—and do just what you desire. Don't worry! It doesn't matter that one or both of you are married to someone else. You must obey your instincts and this delicious feeling of falling in love that's washing over you!' And when the feeling stops and they fall out of love (or one of them does) then they obey that feeling as well. Their feelings are in charge of what they do—and they obey the voice of love. But it isn't true love who is speaking to them.

When we love Christ that brings another power and another presence into our lives. The power of the love of God, who knows always what true love has to do in any situation. Instead of ten commandments carved on stone they are written on hearts of flesh. Written by the Spirit of God on our hearts, and he can do it because he lives in our hearts. John Powell SJ wrote a lovely book entitled *Happiness is an Inside Job*. So is love—and it is the job of the Holy Spirit of God living within us, Counsellor and Comforter and the Spirit of truth. For those disciples that beautiful indwelling by the God of love lay in the future—but not very far in the future. First, the death and resurrection of Christ, then the pouring out of the Spirit of Christ.

A prayer

Lord, teach me how to pray and how to love. Give me the gift of true love—and give me yourself. I know you love me. And I love you—although my love isn't as passionate as I desire it to be. Show me the way to love.

23

John 14:18–20 (NIV)

I will come to you

'I will not leave you as orphans; I will come to you. Before long, the world will not see me any more, but you will see me. Because I live, you also will live. On that day you will realise that I am in my Father, and you are in me, and I am in you.'

As I write these notes the sad little faces of orphaned children look out of our television screens in Britain. There are hundreds of them, in what was once Yugoslavia. The parents who loved them and looked after them are dead—and the people who care for them can never replace their own mothers and fathers.

In the Bible God has a deep compassion for orphans and for widows—and the letter of James says, 'Religion that God our Father accepts as pure and faultless is this: to look after orphans and widows in their distress . . . ' (1:27).

The affliction is that they are not loved and cared for as once they were. The beloved presence has gone away, and the orphans are on their own. But it isn't going to be like that for the followers of Jesus. Neither for the disciples (who had known his physical presence with them) nor for us. 'I will come to you,' Jesus says—and the witness of Christians ever since the beginning has been that he does. An astonishing union and communion takes place. Christ is in the Father, and we are in Christ, and Christ is in us.

A way to pray

O let the Son of God enfold you
With His Spirit and His love,
Let Him fill your heart and satisfy
your soul.
O let Him have the things that hold
you,
And his Spirit like a dove
Will descend upon your life and
make you whole.

John Wimber   (© Mercy Publishing)

John 14:21–24 (NIV)

We will come to you

'Whoever has my commands and obeys them, he is the one who loves me. He who loves me will be loved by my Father, and I too will love him and show myself to him.' Then Judas (not Judas Iscariot) said, 'But, Lord, why do you intend to show yourself to us and not to the world?' Jesus replied, 'If anyone loves me, he will obey my teaching. My Father will love him, and we will come to him and make our home with him. He who does not love me will not obey my teaching. These words you hear are not my own; they belong to the Father who sent me.'

Was Jesus saying that before either he or his Father will love us we have to do just what he tells us and also to love him? If he was then the gospel isn't good news. It's bad. Because we'll never manage either the living or the loving on our own. In his brilliant commentary on John's Gospel, William Temple helps us to understand what this difficult passage really means:

'The Father loves all his children with an infinite love, such love as could be expressed only by giving His only-begotten Son. Yet there is a special love also in His heart for those who love that Son. The universal love of God is not a featureless uniformity of good-will. Good-will to all there is; but also for each whatever special quality of love is appropriate to him; and there must be a special quality of love for those who love the Son whom the Father loved before the foundation of the world. The Son Himself, who is the "express image" of the Father's universal love, has a special quality of love (how could it be otherwise?) for those who love Him in return; and to them He will manifest Himself.' *Readings in St John's Gospel*, Macmillan, 1959.

A prayer
Lord God, I thank you for this amazing truth—that you will make your home in my heart: you who created the galaxies, and our world, and me . . . you who are Father, Son and Holy Spirit, Creator and Lover.

John 14:25–27 (NIV)

The peace of Jesus

'All this I have spoken while still with you. But the Counsellor, the Holy Spirit, whom the Father will send in my name, will teach you all things and will remind you of everything I have said to you. Peace I leave with you; my peace I give you. I do not give to you as the world gives. Do not let your hearts be troubled and do not be afraid.'

The hearts of the disciples *were* troubled—and in view of all the things Jesus had been saying to them it wasn't surprising. He was going away—and they didn't really understand where, even though he told them. And he had spoken of a grain of wheat falling into the ground and dying. It would glorify God in the process and produce many more grains of wheat. But the original grain of wheat wouldn't be there any longer, and neither would Jesus. Not in the same form and not in the same way. No wonder they were troubled. But he knew what was going on in their hearts (he always does) and told them not to be afraid and not to be troubled. They would have a going away present from him. His own special peace. The peace of God which passes all understanding. A peace in which everything is in tune and nothing is out of tune, because all things are in a right relationship with all other things and creatures—and with the Creator God himself. That peace wasn't just for those first followers of Jesus. It was for all of us. Paul discovered it—and knew it even in the midst of his suffering:

'Therefore, since we have been justified through faith, we have peace with God through our Lord Jesus Christ... And we rejoice in the hope of the glory of God. Not only so, but we also rejoice in our sufferings, because we know that suffering produces perseverance; perseverance character; and character, hope. And hope does not disappoint us, because God has poured out his love into our hearts by the Holy Spirit, whom he has given us' (Romans 5:1–5).

A way to pray

Read those verses from Romans slowly—and reflect how one thing leads to another. Is what Paul says true for you?

John 14:28–31 (NIV)

The way to God

'You heard me say, "I am going away and I am coming back to you." If you loved me, you would be glad that I am going to the Father, for the Father is greater than I. I have told you now before it happens, so that when it does happen you will believe. I will not speak with you much longer, for the prince of this world is coming. He has no hold on me, but the world must learn that I love the Father and that I do exactly what my Father has commanded me. Come now; let us leave.'

Jesus is on his way to the Father. But it will be a terrible journey. The way of sorrows, or the *via dolorosa*. What lies ahead is a hideously unjust trial and a hideously unjust death. The evil prince of this world will attack the prince of peace. The one whose name and nature is Abaddon, the destroyer, will try to destroy the Son of God and put out the light of the world.

He won't succeed—but the disciples don't know that yet. They go with him on his way—and as they go he will go on teaching them. Three more chapters that are among the greatest in the whole Bible come between leaving the upper room and the betrayal in the Garden of Gethsemane. But before the resurrection and the pouring out of the Spirit there has to be a death.

A way to pray

Think about Jesus doing exactly what the Father commanded him—and what it cost him. Think about the agony—the death—and then the disciples' desolation. But then think about the wonder of that first Easter morning—and the wonder of Pentecost, when they knew the Christ who died and rose again within their hearts, in the Spirit. Do you know the glory of all those things? If you do, then be thankful...

1 Corinthians 15:21–26 (RSV)

When death dies . . .

For as by a man came death, by a man has come also the resurrection of the dead. For as in Adam all die, so also in Christ shall all be made alive. But each in his own order: Christ the first fruits, then at his coming those who belong to Christ. Then comes the end, when he delivers the kingdom to God the Father after destroying every rule and every authority and power. For he must reign until he has put all his enemies under his feet. The last enemy to be destroyed is death.

The New Testament is not bursting with excitement over a faint hope that Jesus somehow lived on in a spirit world after he died in this one. The excitement and the shouting is about the resurrection of the dead body of Jesus—which will be followed on the resurrection morning by the resurrection of our bodies. 'Jesus and resurrection!' is what the first Christians shouted aloud all over the known world, and some of them went to prison and some of them died because they believed it and preached it, and worshipped as Lord the man who had died and risen from the dead. Jesus Christ—truly God and truly man—who the New Testament writers tell us is reigning on the throne of the universe.

But the One who reigns there knows what it is like to be a human being, because he was one. He knows what it is like to suffer, because he suffered. He knows what it is like to die, because he died. But he also knows what it is like to be raised from the dead—and because we are in Christ so shall we, one day. So when you say the Creed in church today, remember that one day death will be destroyed, and think about the resurrection body, like a glorious plant growing from a seed:

'It is sown in corruption; it is raised in incorruption: It is sown in dishonour; it is raised in glory: it is sown in weakness; it is raised in power: It is sown a natural body; it is raised a spiritual body . . . For this corruptible must put on incorruption, and this mortal must put on immortality. So when this corruptible shall have put on incorruption, and this mortal shall have put on immortality, then shall be brought to pass the saying that is written, Death is swallowed up in victory' (1 Corinthians 15:42–44,53,54 AV).

SB

Psalm 7:12–17 (BCP)

A God-fearing people

God is a righteous Judge, strong, and patient: and God is provoked every day. If a man will not turn, he will whet his sword: he hath bent his bow, and made it ready. He hath prepared for him the instruments of death: he ordaineth his arrows against the persecutors. Behold, he ['the wicked man': RSV] travaileth with mischief: he hath conceived sorrow, and brought forth ungodliness. He hath graven and digged up a pit: and is fallen himself into the destruction that he made for other. For his travail shall come upon his own head: and his wickedness shall fall on his own pate.

No, not a comfortable psalm. A very uncomfortable one. Behind it, however, is a question that clamours to be heard. Does it really matter that by and large the whole idea of God is counted irrelevant? At one time the civilization which Christendom had built up—its laws, its customs and business activities—were grounded in a recognition of the sovereignty of God *over all life*. Not that a moral uprightness was widespread, far from it, but belief in God provided a standard of difference between right and wrong, seen to be neglected at man's peril. In other words, God was to be feared. And this produced a God-fearing people. All this has largely disappeared in the modern world. Indeed, if God is acknowledged at all, it is as a kindly figure ready to let things slide, certainly not One the thought of whom would keep anyone awake.

And then we read this psalm.

Apparently God is provoked every day by what he sees going on in the world. He longs to interfere and punish the wrongdoers, but he holds back. He is 'a righteous judge, strong and patient'. He waits for men and women to turn from their evil ways; and then he will be full of compassion and mercy. But if they do not, if we do not, then... well, dare to read the verses again.

Perhaps you say, 'Oh, but this is *Old* Testament!' But what about this from the New Testament... 'Let us have grace whereby we may serve God acceptably with reverence and godly fear: For our God is a consuming fire' (Hebrews 12:28,29 AV).

A prayer

Lord, make us a God-fearing people through the gospel of your grace

Psalm 10:12–16 (RSV)

The ungodly tyrant

Arise, O Lord; O God, lift up thy hand; forget not the afflicted. Why does the wicked renounce God, and say in his heart, 'Thou wilt not call to account'? Thou dost see; yea, thou dost note trouble and vexation, that thou mayest take it into thy hands; the hapless commits himself to thee; thou hast been the helper of the fatherless. Break thou the arm of the wicked and evildoer; seek out his wickedness till thou find none. The Lord is king for ever and ever; the nations shall perish from his land.

As I write this I see in my mind's eye pictures of terrified mothers with babies in arms fleeing from Sarajevo; I see Kurdish families struggling up into the mountains only to face hunger and cold; I see emaciated children by the thousand staring pitifully out of sunken eyes in the Horn of Africa. And behind all these heart-breaking scenes is some tyrant crazy for power no matter what price in human misery. Is it any wonder that the great cry goes up, everywhere—'O God WHY?' Or as verse 1 has it, 'Why dost thou stand afar off, O Lord? Why dost thou hide thyself in times of trouble?'

The trouble with tyrants is that they do not think wrongdoing is ever punished. But tyrants are not the only men and women with these views. There are Christians who gloss over what Paul writes in Romans 11:22: 'Behold then the goodness and *severity* of God.' But if God were indifferent to wrongdoing then to appeal to him, to pray to him, would be useless. The psalmist, however, in today's verses did cry out to God, even if the word 'Why' did occupy a large part of his prayer. Even so, he ended on a note of confidence, 'The Lord is king for ever and ever ... O Lord, thou wilt hear the desire of the meek; thou wilt strengthen their heart, thou wilt incline thy ear to do justice to the fatherless and the oppressed, so that man who is of the earth may strike terror no more.'

A prayer
Lord, the cry of the world's pain is baffling to faith in you. Lord, where I cannot see, help me to hold on.

Psalm 15 (RSV)

The man of God

O Lord, who shall sojourn in thy tent? Who shall dwell on thy holy hill? He who walks blamelessly, and does what is right, and speaks truth from his heart; who does not slander with his tongue, and does no evil to his friend, nor takes up a reproach against his neighbour; in whose eyes a reprobate is despised, but who honours those who fear the Lord; who swears to his own hurt and does not change; who does not put out his money at interest, and does not take a bribe against the innocent. He who does these things shall never be moved.

I disliked the headmaster of my school intensely. His policy was to keep order by terrorizing us boys. This was foolish. Some boys need a heavy hand, others need encouragement. Not surprisingly, I only remember one thing he ever said. It was about Psalm 15 and he called it the gentleman's psalm. 'If we followed its precepts,' he said, 'we really would be gentlemen.'

Well! This is not why I am inviting you to think over this psalm, but rather because it describes the genuine man of God, and in practical, down-to-earth terms, actions and attitudes for the ordinary world of day-to-day living, out and about among people. Psalm 15 is by no means the preserve of sanctuaries and places of spiritual retreat, though it should be lived out there.

The first emphasis is on doing— 'He who walks blamelessly, and does what is right': in other words, integrity. This is not a characteristic of today's world. Moral chaos is everywhere, goaded by individualism and 'everybody does it'. And then truthfulness in speech. Where do the politicians, the advertisers and the salesmen come in this? Who can we believe today? And then money. Some people will do anything for money, but not the man of God.

What a better place the world would be if Psalm 15 were followed! And the lesson for us? We cannot know God's presence if we are fiddlers with words, deeds or money.

A prayer

Lord, we seek your face. Keep from us all that would block our vision.

Acts 1:3–9 (NIV)

The promise of the Spirit

After his suffering, he [Jesus] showed himself to these men and gave many convincing proofs that he was alive. He appeared to them over a period of forty days and spoke about the kingdom of God. On one occasion, while he was eating with them, he gave them this command: 'Do not leave Jerusalem, but wait for the gift my Father promised, which you have heard me speak about. For John baptised with water, but in a few days you will be baptised with the Holy Spirit.' So when they met together, they asked him, 'Lord, are you at this time going to restore the kingdom to Israel?' He said to them: 'It is not for you to know the times or dates the Father has set by his own authority. But you will receive power when the Holy Spirit comes on you; and you will be my witnesses in Jerusalem, and in all Judea and Samaria, and to the ends of the earth.' After he said this, he was taken up before their very eyes, and a cloud hid him from their sight.

We do not have many details about the forty days between the Resurrection and the Ascension. But the records tell us that Jesus was alive. He appeared to his disciples, and he talked and ate with them. He spent time teaching them eternal truths 'about the kingdom of God'. But even now they were short sighted, concerned for a temporal kingdom in Israel. We can deplore their lack of understanding. But is our own focus on man's world or on God's?

Then, just before the Ascension, Jesus told the disciples what to do next. The instructions were clear: 'Wait in Jerusalem.' The promise was clear: 'You will be given the Holy Spirit.' The Spirit would give them new power. He would enable them to say of Jesus, 'I know, because I have experienced . . .' He would send them to share the good news, first with their neighbours, then more widely over the world. As we read Acts we see how excitingly this worked out in the next decade and more.

A reflection

Do I know the power of the Holy Spirit in my life? Am I concerned to be a witness of Jesus in this Decade of Evangelism?

Acts 1:21–26 (NIV)

Making decisions

'It is necessary to choose one of the men who have been with us the whole time the Lord Jesus went in and out among us, beginning from John's baptism to the time when Jesus was taken up from us. For one of these must become a witness of his resurrection.' So they proposed two men: Joseph called Barsabbas (also known as Justus) and Matthias. Then they prayed, 'Lord, you know everyone's heart. Show us which of these two you have chosen to take over this apostolic ministry, which Judas has left to go where he belongs.' Then they cast lots, and the lot fell to Matthias; so he was added to the eleven apostles.

One day Peter spoke to the larger group of 120 believers about the need to replace Judas among the Twelve. The person chosen would need two qualifications: he must have been a follower of Jesus ever since the beginning of his ministry, and he must have seen Jesus after his resurrection.

They set us a good example in their decision-making. The decision was made corporately, by the whole group. They used their minds to see who were the possible candidates. They prayed, appealing to the Lord's insight and direction. They trusted God. It seems strange to us that they should draw lots, but for them it was an accepted practice. Their prayer shows that they were not appealing to chance, but they were trusting God to overrule the way the lot fell.

A reflection and a prayer

Think about your way of making decisions. Do you decide alone or consult others? Do you use your mind to weigh up the situation? Do you pray and submit your thinking to God? Do you trust the sovereign God to be in charge of all that happens? Then pray:
Lord, I look back and confess that I have often left you out of my decision-making, and pray for your forgiveness and my ability to change. So now I think about the decisions that are facing me . . . (be specific about your own situation . . .). I ask that I may see how to follow the way those early Christians went about it.

Psalm 31:18–20,24 (RSV)

Malicious gossip

Let the lying lips be dumb, which speak insolently against the righteous in pride and contempt. O how abundant is thy goodness, which thou hast laid up for those who fear thee, and wrought for those who take refuge in thee, in the sight of the sons of men! In the covert of thy presence thou hidest them from the plots of men; thou holdest them safe under thy shelter from the strife of tongues . . . Be strong, and let your heart take courage, all you who wait for the Lord!

If I close my eyes I can see a vivid picture of my mother standing before the kitchen range. She was holding up the local newspaper (I think it was the *Eastern Daily Press*) and reading the inside pages. Suddenly, she gasped out loud and looked very frightened. I was only about ten years old and was greatly alarmed. I did not know what to do, for she screwed up the paper and with it rapidly quitted the kitchen. I followed, but she had gone to her bedroom. Boylike, of course, I searched everywhere for that newspaper. But I never found it. And she did not tell me what her eyes had seen there till years later. It was a report of her brother being sent to prison for three months for embezzling some money.

The horror and shame of this hurt her terribly. She had become a regular churchgoer and she feared the malicious gossip of the neighbourhood and the gibes that might be made about her own Christian profession.

But in church she had come to know the psalms, and verse 20 of our reading today brought her through: 'In the covert of thy presence thou hidest them from the plots of men; thou holdest them safe under thy shelter from the strife of tongues.'

It is not only deeds that can hurt us when we are down. So can cruel words. But we can pray for God's protection. My mother did this and found it. There was no gossip.

A prayer
Lord, when things go badly with me, or with the people I love, protect me, and my faith, from unkind words and cruel tongues.

Mark 14:22–25 (RSV)

Commitment

And as they were eating, he took bread, and blessed, and broke it, and gave it to them, and said, 'Take; this is my body.' And he took a cup, and when he had given thanks he gave it to them, and they all drank of it. And he said to them, 'This is my blood of the covenant, which is poured out for many. Truly, I say to you, I shall not drink again of the fruit of the vine until that day when I drink it new in the kingdom of God.'

Perhaps it is a pity we cannot see the faces of these men at table. My guess is that bewilderment was stamped all over them. Inquiringly, they looked hard at each other! What does he mean? What is our Master doing? They were all busily eating. The account says so. Then he took a piece of bread, gave a blessing and broke it and gave it to them. He told them to take it. He said the bread was his body. It did not look in the least like his body. Then the cup. 'This is my blood of the covenant which is poured out for many.' His blood? Did this mean a sacrificial death? At this very table? And then these enigmatic words following, 'I shall not drink again of the fruit of the vine.' To assert that these men did not understand is almost too inept a comment to be worth passing. Nevertheless we make it. The disciples of Jesus took the bread and the wine although they did not understand. They did it because their Lord and Master told them to do so, and because he said they were his body and his blood.

A few days ago I read of a young man who said he could not partake of the Holy Communion because he did not understand what was being done there, and what was being offered and taken. He was an intelligent young man. Are you going to blame him? Perhaps he had heard phrases used in this connection such as 'Real Presence' and 'Transubstantiation' and 'Epiklesis'. But there are some things that can only be understood if you do them. Falling in love is one such. Externally viewed it is irrational, almost stupid. But commitment changes everything. So with the Holy Communion. The mind is not out of place here but the heart has the chief place.

DCF

Psalm 104:10–18 (RSV)

God's creatures

Thou makest springs gush forth in the valleys; they flow between the hills, they give drink to every beast of the field; the wild asses quench their thirst. By them the birds of the air have their habitation; they sing among the branches. From thy lofty abode thou waterest the mountains; the earth is satisfied with the fruit of thy work. Thou dost cause the grass to grow for the cattle, and plants for man to cultivate, that he may bring forth food from the earth, and wine to gladden the heart of man, oil to make his face shine, and bread to strengthen man's heart. The trees of the Lord are watered abundantly, the cedars of Lebanon which he planted. In them the birds build their nests; the stork has her home in the fir trees. The high mountains are for the wild goats; the rocks are a refuge for the badgers.

As I write this a blackbird is singing his head off in the silver birch tree just outside my study window. Because his song is out in the open we do not realize how powerful it is. Had he perched inside the house I should have had to plug my ears. But the birdsong is meant to be heard by other birds at a distance. All this the author of Psalm 104 would say is the design of God the Creator. The birds are his and he has provided for them, and for the cattle, the wild goats and the badgers. And we are bracketed with birds and animals as far as the Creator's provision is concerned; wine to make our hearts glad and oil to polish up our faces. Well, this is not quite how we would express it! But let us not miss the point. The Bible talks about God's provision whereas we talk about Nature's provision and leave God out; or else assume that God and Nature are the same which is definitely not what the Bible teaches.

The world of Nature certainly is wonderful. Modern television programmes reveal the wonders as never before but we must not deify nature. It is God's creation and the animals are God's creatures and it is our special duty *as human beings* to praise God for his creation.

A prayer

Lord, I thank you for that blackbird and all the rich variety of nature that you have given us. Praise be to you the wonderful Creator.

Psalm 107:8–14 (BCP)

The empty soul

O that men would therefore praise the Lord for his goodness: and declare the wonders that he doeth for the children of men! For he satisfieth the empty soul: and filleth the hungry soul with goodness. Such as sit in darkness, and in the shadow of death: being fast bound in misery and iron; Because they rebelled against the words of the Lord: and lightly regarded the counsel of the most Highest; He also brought down their heart through heaviness: they fell down and there was none to help them. So when they cried unto the Lord in their trouble: he delivered them out of their distress. For he brought them out of darkness, and out of the shadow of death: and brake their bonds in sunder.

I wonder if you have ever said sadly of someone you know, 'I am afraid there isn't much in him (or in her).' I was reading the other day about a young man who produced just that reaction in me. His life-style had consisted of fast motor cars, late night parties, the most up-to-date fashions in food and drink and an apparently endless series of girl-friends. Altogether an empty life. And it all indicated an empty soul. There was a photograph of him at that stage in his life and I could read it in his face. The eyes and the mouth told of utter boredom. It is not difficult to understand how such poor people (and they are poor, though well supplied with money) can commit suicide. Meaninglessness kills them.

But then something happened to this young man. He became a caring, diligent family man. People were surprised. The man with 'nothing in him' began to exhibit sheer goodness. It all happened after he experienced a personal loss that really hurt. The distress came first. Then the deliverance.

Now read today's verses again. Don't they begin to take on meaning?

Sad to say there are crowds of empty people in our modern world. Some have never known what it is to have to 'go without'. Contentment does not come that way. Maybe some form of hardship will have to be experienced before they will know it. Today's psalm tells us that God satisfies the empty soul. What a wonder! What a promise!

A prayer

Lord, I pray for . . . and for . . . and for those who do not seem to have found any real satisfaction in life.

Psalm 122:1–2,6,7 (RSV)

Uplifting worship

I was glad when they said to me, 'Let us go to the house of the Lord!'
Our feet have been standing within your gates, O Jerusalem!
Jerusalem, built as a city which is bound firmly together . . . Pray for
the peace of Jerusalem! 'May they prosper who love you! Peace be
within your walls, and security within your towers.'

It is almost impossible for me to read these verses without hearing in my mind the music of Parry's magnificent anthem entitled 'I was glad'. But a recording of the music, or even hearing it broadcast live over the radio, does not compare with actually being present when it is sung on some great occasion. It is the cathedral packed with worshippers—hundreds of individuals all united in one superb act of praise—that takes hold and lifts the whole congregation out of itself up onto a higher plane. This is what corporate worship should accomplish. And if we thought that attendance would translate this into a reality for us wouldn't we echo the opening words of this psalm?—'I was glad when they said to me, "Let us go to the house of the Lord."' Worship should bring us into the presence of God. It should also lift us up out of our little selves. Don't write this off as mere emotion. Religion without feeling is barren. It will accomplish very little.

And note this. Our acts of corporate worship on one day of the week will deepen our awareness of God's sovereignty and care over our lives *every* day and *every* week, busy as we may be with multifarious activities. I put one critical question therefore about an act of worship in church on Sunday. Was it uplifting? Will the impression still be there on Monday morning? Now be honest!

Read the rest of today's verses. The Church should be at unity in itself, division and quarrels kept at bay. We should pray for our church, our local church. God adds his blessing to all who care deeply about its welfare.

A prayer

Lord, we need more organists and choristers today, more musicians and singers, men and women of musical accomplishment and Christian dedication. Lord, hear our prayer.

Psalm 134 (RSV)

A prayer vigil

Come, bless the Lord, all you servants of the Lord, who stand by night in the house of the Lord! Lift up your hands to the holy place, and bless the Lord! May the Lord bless you from Zion, he who made heaven and earth!

There are two necessities if we are to make much sense of this psalm, namely information and imagination. It can so easily roll off our tongues as mere words, well, mine anyway. The temple in Jerusalem was kept open all day, every day, for prayer and worship, but at night it was closed. Not only closed, but guarded. There was a temple watch. Before, however, the priests locked them in they called to them bidding them to lift up their hands in the sanctuary and praise the Lord. So these temple night watchmen were not mere security guards. They were the servants of the Lord with a ministry to perform. They were to see that the prayers to God never ceased in the temple, neither by day nor by night. They were to be continuous. And with the call to these night watchmen to pray there came back the answer to the call--'May the Lord bless you from Zion, he who made heaven and earth.' There is a reward for those who maintain the prayer service whether it be day or night.

This is not an activity most of us can engage in all day long. There are a thousand and one mundane duties to perform and I certainly could not possibly keep awake all night for prayer, not even one night! What this psalm does for me is to remind me that throughout every twenty-four hours, always, I am in God's hands. He is the Lord and I am safe there. I acknowledge this even if I cannot always be expressing it in words. The best I can manage is a short reminder in the morning before I start work and in the evening before I go to sleep. But on the basis of this psalm I believe God will add his blessing to this little service of mine, and yours too.

A prayer

We praise thee, O God, we acknowledge thee to be the Lord.

From the *Te Deum* (BCP)

Psalm 118:19–24 (RSV)

Marvellous in our eyes

Open to me the gates of righteousness, that I may enter through them and give thanks to the Lord. This is the gate of the Lord; the righteous shall enter through it. I thank thee that thou hast answered me and hast become my salvation. The stone which the builders rejected has become the head of the corner. This is the Lord's doing; it is marvellous in our eyes. This is the day which the Lord has made; let us rejoice and be glad in it.

Perhaps you are hurrying off to work or sitting in the commuter train, which you use for your 'quiet time before God' (and why not?). How can you be expected to give your mind to what happened at the rebuilding of the Jewish Temple after the Jewish people returned from that devastating exile following that devastating defeat in war, all centuries before Christ? Perhaps, though, if I tell you a little you will experience something like turning on a light in a dark cupboard. Today's verses sound all right, but what do they mean? Let me tell you.

The great procession of priests and people had just reached the gates of the newly restored temple. 'Open to me the gates of righteousness,' cried the leader, 'that I may enter through them and give thanks to the Lord.' And those waiting to receive them called out 'This is the gate of the Lord, the righteous shall enter through it.' And then, looking up, they marvelled to see the rebuilt and restored temple—built of the very same stones that had lain around in ruins for years, stones which they had thought of as useless. Wonderful! Marvellous! 'This is the Lord's doing. It is marvellous in our eyes. This is the day which the Lord has made; let us rejoice and be glad in it.'

Perhaps we have experienced great days like this. And for Christians the greatest of all is Easter Day, the day on which the rejected and crucified Christ was raised to life again to be the foundation stone of the worldwide Church. 'It is marvellous in our eyes'! Never lose the wonder of this, not even if your prayer time happens to be in the train or lying in a sickbed. There is wonder at the heart of our faith.

A prayer

Lord, you are a God who does marvels. Open my eyes to see them, sometimes in the most unexpected places.

Psalm 149 (RSV)

A new song

Praise the Lord! Sing to the Lord a new song, his praise in the assembly of the faithful! Let Israel be glad in his Maker, let the sons of Zion rejoice in their King! Let them praise his name with dancing, making melody to him with timbrel and lyre! For the Lord takes pleasure in his people; he adorns the humble with victory. Let the faithful exult in glory; let them sing for joy on their couches. Let the high praises of God be in their throats and two-edged swords in their hands, to wreak vengeance on the nations and chastisement on the peoples, to bind their kings with chains and their nobles with fetters of iron, to execute on them the judgment written! This is glory for all his faithful ones. Praise the Lord!

We can sing this psalm quite merrily to start with. But then all of a sudden we stop. We can't sing the rest as Christians, can we? But I have included these verses in order to be honest. You would distrust me as a commentator if I kept only to the attractive bits. I am not going to explain these verses away. After the restoration of Israel in the time of Ezra and Nehemiah, when this psalm was probably written, the nation *did* want to hit back at those who had hit them. We know that this is not in accordance with the Spirit of Christ. But some Christians have not been open about this. Using these very verses the Thirty Years War was started, a terrible bloody conflict in Germany. And Thomas Munzer appealed to the same verses when he stirred up the Peasants' War.

There now. I have got that off my chest. So the new song. What was it? The old song was the one they had been singing for ages to commemorate the deliverance from Egypt. But now there was a new deliverance to celebrate. Is this not so with us? We have had great deliverances in our lives in the past. But what about last week, or even yesterday? Haven't we a new song to sing of God's goodness to us?

A prayer

Lord, you have led me through many rough places. Here's my new song.

41

Introduction to Acts

This book is just called Acts. We often think of it as the Acts of the Apostles, but it would be better named the Acts of the Holy Spirit, without whom the apostles were timid and ineffectual.

Earlier this year we read from chapters 8 to 18 of this book. Now we are going back to enjoy the story of the Holy Spirit's coming at Pentecost in this season of the church's year. May this Pentecost season have new meaning for each of us.

Acts could also be called the Acts of the Early Church. We read of infant churches with more vitality and zeal than many of our own churches nowadays. These first seven chapters are about the church in Jerusalem.

As I said in March, in the introduction to chapters 8 to 18, the key verse of Acts is found in Jesus' last recorded words to his disciples.

'You will receive power when the Holy Spirit comes on you; and you will be my witnesses in Jerusalem, and in all Judea and Samaria, and to the ends of the earth' (Acts 1:8).

This is a vital verse for the Decade of Evangelism. We can learn it by heart, pray it in our heart, and then do what it promises.

Rosemary Green

Acts 2:1–13 (NIV)

Invaded by the Spirit

When the day of Pentecost came, they were all together in one place. Suddenly a sound like the blowing of a violent wind came from heaven and filled the whole house where they were sitting. They saw what seemed to be tongues of fire that separated and came to rest on each of them. All of them were filled with the Holy Spirit and began to speak in other tongues as the Spirit enabled them. Now there were staying in Jerusalem God-fearing Jews from every nation under heaven. When they heard this sound, a crowd came together in bewilderment, because each one heard them speaking in his own language. Utterly amazed, they asked: 'Are not all these men who are speaking Galileans? Then how is it that each of us hears them in his own native language? . . . we hear them declaring the wonders of God in our own tongues!' Amazed and perplexed, they asked one another, 'What does this mean?' Some, however, made fun of them and said, 'They have had too much wine.'

Jesus' followers prayed and waited for the promised Holy Spirit. His arrival was unmistakable! Things began to happen. The wind filled the house, and the Spirit's presence could be felt all round them. Flames were seen on each individual, and each person was touched. They began to speak in 'tongues'. God gives this gift to many Christians today—either a known language to convey God's message, or unknown words to enrich prayer. A clergyman I know once spoke in tongues during a sermon. An amazed visitor in the congregation asked 'How does he know High German?' God used this means to catch the person's attention. The people praised God freely as they 'declared his wonders'. (I was a Christian for many years before the Spirit's fresh touch gave me real joy in worship.) Reactions were mixed—honest enquiry or sceptical mocking.

The same happens nowadays. The Spirit does not always work so dramatically. He may come more like a breeze than a gale. But when he comes we shall still see clear evidence of his powerful activity.

A way to pray

Dare you ask God to release his Spirit in you? Can you let him choose how he does it?

RG

Acts 2:14–21 (NIV)

The Bible comes alive

Then Peter stood up with the Eleven, raised his voice and addressed the crowd: 'Fellow Jews and all of you who live in Jerusalem. Let me explain this to you; listen carefully to what I say. These men are not drunk . . . It's only nine in the morning! No, this is what was spoken by the prophet Joel: "In the last days, God says, I will pour out my Spirit on all people. Your sons and your daughters will prophesy, your young men will see visions, your old men will dream dreams . . . I will show wonders in the heaven above and signs on the earth below . . . And everyone who calls on the name of the Lord will be saved".'

Do you remember Peter's cowardice when Jesus was on trial? Three times he denied any association with Jesus. What a transformation when the Spirit came! In the face of charges of drunkenness he stood up with the other eleven disciples and preached a bold, impromptu sermon. He first addressed the mockers: 'No, we are not drunk. The Spirit has come.'

The Spirit gave Peter a new understanding of Scripture. He quoted first from the prophet Joel and later on from Psalms 16 and 110. He proclaimed that their new experience was fulfilling Joel's words that the Spirit would be poured out on all believers, not just on a select few (as in the Old Testament). Peter expected the prophecies, visions, dreams, wonders and signs that all follow in the Book of Acts.

The Spirit enabled Peter to recall whole passages of Scripture. The Jews were strong on memorizing—and we can take a leaf out of their book. We can learn parts of the Bible by heart, ready for the Spirit to prompt us in times of need. The Spirit also enhances our own love of Scripture. He can give us a new hunger for the Bible and new joy and understanding in reading it.

A prayer

Blessed Lord, who caused all holy Scriptures to be written for our learning: help us to hear them, to read, mark, learn and inwardly digest them that, through patience and the comfort of your holy word, we may embrace and for ever hold fast the hope of everlasting life, which you have given us in our Saviour Jesus Christ.

The Collect for the second Sunday in Advent, ASB

Acts 2:22–24,32,33 (NIV)

Peter's message

'Men of Israel, listen to this: Jesus of Nazareth was a man accredited by God to you by miracles, wonders and signs, which God did among you through him, as you yourselves know. This man was handed over to you by God's set purpose and fore-knowledge; and you, with the help of wicked men, put him to death by nailing him to the cross. But God raised him from the dead, freeing him from the agony of death, because it was impossible for death to keep its hold on him . . . God has raised this Jesus to life, and we are all witnesses of the fact. Exalted to the right hand of God, he has received from the Father the promised Holy Spirit and has poured out what you now see and hear.'

After responding to the mockers Peter spoke about the heart of his good news, Jesus: who lived, died, rose and ascended.

Jesus who lived. 'Jesus of Nazareth' was human, but 'accredited by God': divine power was demonstrated in his works. Peter reminds his hearers that Jesus' deeds were not mere hearsay; even those who had not watched Jesus' deeds could see their effects. *Jesus who died.* 'You...put him to death.' Peter puts the responsibility for the cross onto his hearers, along with the traitor Judas and the jealous Jewish and Roman leaders. Yet behind these men was 'God's set purpose and foreknow-ledge'. Isn't it utterly amazing? God knew from the beginning that human disobedience would spoil his good creation. Yet he actually used human wickedness in his divine plan to redeem human wickedness. *Jesus who rose.* Immediately after the crucifixion the

disciples must have been altogether confused and discouraged. But then they saw Jesus alive—and on one occasion 'he appeared to more than five hundred... at the same time' (1 Corinthians 15:6). So the resurrection became a linchpin of the apostles' preaching. *Jesus who ascended.* After they had waited in Jerusalem, as he told them to just before the Ascension, Jesus fulfilled his promise that his followers would be enriched when he left them and the Spirit came to them.

A reflection

Peter wrote later that we should be ready to explain our faith to everyone who asks us about it (1 Peter 3:15). Are you more ready to speak about church activity—or about Jesus who lived, died and rose, and whose Spirit is resident in your life?

Acts 2:36–41 (NIV)

A challenge to commitment

'Therefore let all be Israel be assured of this: God has made this Jesus, whom you crucified, both Lord and Christ.' When the people heard this, they were cut to the heart and said to Peter and the other apostles, 'Brothers, what shall we do?' Peter replied, 'Repent and be baptised, every one of you, in the name of Jesus Christ for the forgiveness of your sins. And you will receive the gift of the Holy Spirit. The promise is for you and your children and for all who are far off—for all whom the Lord our God will call.' With many other words he warned them; and he pleaded with them, 'Save yourselves from this corrupt generation.' Those who accepted his message were baptised, and about three thousand were added to their number that day.

Peter's sermon, inspired by the Holy Spirit, was direct and hard-hitting. The hearers were 'cut to the heart' by the words and by the Spirit, whom Jesus had said would 'convict the world of guilt' (John 16:8). Their cry was 'Help! What are we to do?' Peter's answer was quite clear. *They had to repent.* Repentance means a change of direction. If they were to receive forgiveness for sins they needed to turn round from those sins. *They had to be baptized.* This was a public declaration of the commitment of their wills and hearts. *They would be given the Holy Spirit.* That is the right of all people who commit themselves to Jesus' way. Peter said that the promise was for his hearers, for their children and for all whom God would call. This does not mean that the children of believers are automatically children of faith; they, like others who will hear about Jesus, are each responsible for their own commitment, even if they have been baptized as infants. Personal response *and* baptism are important Christian foundations, whichever happens first.

A question
How does this passage challenge you?

Acts 2:42–47 (NIV)

A living fellowship

They devoted themselves to the apostles' teaching and to the fellowship, to the breaking of bread and to prayer. Everyone was filled with awe, and many wonders and miraculous signs were done by the apostles. All the believers were together and had everything in common. Selling their possessions and goods, they gave to anyone as he had need. Every day they continued to meet together in the temple courts. They broke bread in their homes and ate together with glad and sincere hearts, praising God and enjoying the favour of all the people. And the Lord added to their number daily those who were being saved.

Daily growth in our church! That would be exciting—so long as we were flexible, willing to change to accommodate the growth. What were the marks of this church in Jerusalem which 'enjoyed the favour of all the people' and attracted so many to join the believers? *They devoted themselves*... That implies wholehearted commitment. *...to the apostles' teaching*... These new believers were hungry to learn from Old Testament Scripture and from all the apostles had learnt from Jesus. *...to the fellowship*... They were not individualistic in their faith, as many of us are. *...to the breaking of bread*... The Eucharist was central. They had no church buildings but met for worship in their own homes. *...to prayer*... This apparently included formal, traditional prayer in the temple and public Christian worship in the temple courtyard as well as solo and corporate prayer in their homes.

Everyone was filled with awe... They had a great awareness of God's presence and reverence for him. *There were many miracles*... The disciples had watched Jesus, and now, empowered by the Spirit, they copied him. *They held their possessions loosely*... They did not say 'mine' but 'ours'. *They shared meals together with glad and sincere hearts*... They loved being together in joy and openness. *They were full of praise*...

A reflection and a prayer

Think *How far does my life and my church's life match up to those early Christians?* **Pray** *Most merciful Redeemer, Friend and Brother, may we know you more clearly, love you more dearly, and follow you more nearly, day by day.*

Richard, Bishop of Chichester

Acts 3:1–10 (NIV)

A miracle of healing

One day Peter and John were going up to the temple at the time of prayer—at three in the afternoon. Now a man crippled from birth was being carried to the temple gate called Beautiful, where he was put every day to beg from those going into the temple courts. When he saw Peter and John about to enter, he asked them for money. Peter looked straight at him, as did John. Then Peter said, 'Look at us!' So the man gave them his attention, expecting to get something from them. Then Peter said, 'Silver or gold I do not have, but what I have I give you. In the name of Jesus Christ of Nazareth, walk.' Taking him by the right hand, he helped him up, and instantly the man's feet and ankles became strong. He jumped to his feet and began to walk. Then he went with them into the temple courts, walking and jumping, and praising God. When all the people saw him walking and praising God, they recognised him as the same man who used to sit begging at the temple gate called Beautiful, and they were filled with wonder and amazement at what had happened to him.

Imagine the scene, and put yourself in the place of the lame man. Think how he felt as he was carried to his regular begging spot; as he asked for money; as he was told to get up and walk; as Peter took his hand; as he went into the temple courtyard; as the crowd watched in amazement. Take pen and paper (later, if you can't do it now), and 'be' the cripple writing your diary that evening. Use this to sense the power of Jesus making an impact on your life.

This man had been incapacitated for forty years. That fact encouraged me ten years ago when I was struggling with the effects of lifelong pain and anger—and I was over forty years old. I thought 'If God could heal *that* man, he can change *me!*' He did. The power of Christ is still active. This morning I prayed for the same power to overcome a chronic bad habit left over from childhood.

For prayer
Talk to God about anything that has troubled you for many years, and ask for the power of Christ for change.

Acts 4:1–4 (NIV)

Weakness and power

The priests and the captain of the temple guard and the Sadducees came up to Peter and John while they were speaking to the people. They were greatly disturbed because the apostles were teaching the people and proclaiming in Jesus the resurrection of the dead. They seized Peter and John, and because it was evening, they put them in jail until the next day. But many who heard the message believed, and the number of men grew to about five thousand.

Peter and John had gone to the temple for the formal time of prayer. Some might have thought that a major miracle was enough excitement for one day. But Peter was immediately ready to talk to the gathering crowds about Jesus. He reminded them plainly that they were responsible for killing Jesus, 'the author of life'. But this Jesus was raised from the dead by their nation's God, and it was 'by faith in the name of Jesus' that the cripple was healed. 'When God raised up his servant, he sent him first to you to bless you by turning each of you from your wicked ways' (Acts 3:26). Peter sets us an example in his readiness to seize any opportunity to talk about Jesus, and in the boldness and clarity of his message.

The reactions to his preaching were strong. On one hand hundreds more joined the crowd of believers. On the other hand there was strong antagonism. That is always so. The more clearly the gospel is preached, the more it divides followers from sceptics. The opposing groups had different motives. Look again to see why they were 'greatly disturbed'. The priests would have been fearful of losing their authority with the ordinary people. The Christians threatened them as much as Jesus did. The Sadducees would have been outraged by any suggestion that the resurrection could be true. And the captain of the temple guard would have been concerned for security and order in the temple precincts—and probably for his own job security too. So out of their weakness they used their power to imprison the apostles.

A reflection

Think about yourself, your priorities and your fears. Then consider each of the people in this story, and decide whom you are most like. Peter? The new believers? The priests? The Sadducees? The captain?

49

Ephesians 1:3–4,12–14 (NIV)

Three in One

Praise be to the God and Father of our Lord Jesus Christ, who has blessed us in the heavenly realms with every spiritual blessing in Christ. For he chose us in him before the creation of the world to be holy and blameless in his sight... in order that we, who were the first to hope in Christ, might be for the praise of his glory. And you also were included in Christ when you heard the word of truth, the gospel of your salvation. Having believed, you were marked in him with a seal, the promised Holy Spirit, who is a deposit guaranteeing our inheritance.

If we have trouble with the Trinity then the best way to troubleshoot is to pray. And even if we don't find the doctrine a difficulty then the best way to experience the reality of it in our hearts is still to pray.

Start with a prayer of praise: 'Praise be to the God and Father of our Lord Jesus Christ, who has blessed us in the heavenly realms with every spiritual blessing in Christ...' Then reflect on the relationship which Jesus had with God: a life of unbroken communion between the Father and the Son. Sometimes Jesus got up very early, to pray to his 'Abba', the child's word for a father. The Father is God—and Jesus is the Lord—and the Father is not the Son and the Son is not the Father. We can reflect on that—and remember how the Son taught his disciples (and us) to pray ... 'When you pray, say "Our Father ..."' We can let a deep thankfulness well up in our hearts as we let the love flow between us and God. And as we worship we realise the source of the bless-

ing: 'God ... who has blessed us in the heavenly realms with every spiritual blessing in Christ.' It was the first Christians who first experienced the wonder of that blessing, and God had a purpose and a plan in mind: 'For he chose us ... in order that we, who were the first to hope in Christ, might be for the praise of his glory ...' They were to 'be' people from whom the glory of God shone out—so that when other people looked at their lives they saw something of what God showed to the world in Jesus: 'the glory of God in the face of Christ' (2 Corinthians 4:6). Jesus is like God, and those first Christians were called to be like him as well.

But not only them: 'You also were included in Christ when you heard the word of truth, the gospel of your salvation. Having believed, you were marked in him with a seal, the promised Holy Spirit, who is a deposit guaranteeing our inheritance until the redemption of those who are God's possession—to the praise of his glory.'

SB

Acts 4:5–13,18–20 (NIV)

Weakness and courage

The next day the rulers, elders and teachers of the law met in Jerusalem . . . They had Peter and John brought before them and began to question them: 'By what power or what name did you do this?' Then Peter, filled with the Holy Spirit, said to them: '. . . If we are being called to account today for an act of kindness shown to a cripple and are asked how he was healed, then know this . . . It is by the name of Jesus Christ of Nazareth, whom you crucified but whom God raised from the dead, that this man stands before you healed . . . Salvation is found in no-one else, for there is no other name under heaven given to men by which we must be saved.' When they saw the courage of Peter and John and realised that they were unschooled, ordinary men, they were astonished and they took note that these men had been with Jesus . . . [The leaders then conferred on their own] . . . Then they called them in again and commanded them not to speak or teach at all in the name of Jesus. But Peter and John replied, 'Judge for yourselves whether it is right in God's sight to obey you rather than God. For we cannot help speaking about what we have seen and heard.'

The Jewish leaders were in a quandary. They had hoped that Jesus' death would end their difficulties. Now they found themselves facing new problems! They knew the healing was real and that 'all the people were praising God for what had happened' (v. 21). Two ordinary men stood before them, and the whole group of leaders was floored.

A promise

'When they arrest you, do not worry about what to say or how to say it. At that time you will be given what to say, for it will not be you speaking, but the Spirit of your Father speaking through you' (Matthew 10:19–20).

A prayer

Lord Jesus, I confess that I fail in my courage to speak for you, and in . . . [fill in your own words]. Please fill me with your Spirit, that I may be more like Peter and John, and more . . .

51

Acts 4:23–31 (NIV)

Bold prayer

On their release, Peter and John went back to their own people and reported all that the chief priests and elders had said to them. When they heard this, they raised their voices together in prayer to God. 'Sovereign Lord,' they said, 'you made the heaven and the earth and the sea, and everything in them. You spoke by the Holy Spirit through the mouth of your servant, our father David: 'Why do the nations rage and the peoples plot in vain? The kings of the earth take their stand and the rulers gather together against the Lord and against his Anointed One.' Indeed Herod and Pontius Pilate met together with the Gentiles and the people of Israel in this city to conspire against your holy servant Jesus whom you anointed. They did what your power and will had decided beforehand should happen. Now, Lord, consider their threats and enable your servants to speak your word with great boldness. Stretch out your hand to heal and perform miraculous signs and wonders through the name of your holy servant Jesus.'

Set free, Peter and John returned to their friends; 'They told us to stop preaching.' Most of us would spend hours discussing the situation, but they immediately prayed. Notice how they praised God: *Sovereign Lord*: God is in total control. *You made*: He is Lord of all creation. *You spoke by the Holy Spirit*. I believe they had in mind the whole of Psalm 2, which continues, 'The One enthroned in heaven laughs… he rebukes them in his anger…' God is Lord over all rulers. *Your power and will had decided*: Even the conspiracy against Jesus was in God's eternal purpose. Now notice their requests.

Enable your servants to speak: even though it was Peter's preaching that put them in prison! *Stretch out your hand to heal*: even though it was a miracle that started the fuss. Then, 'After they prayed, the place where they were meeting was shaken. And they were all filled with the Holy Spirit and spoke the word of God boldly.' (v. 31)

A reflection
Consider how you are feeling now. How does that make you want to pray?

Acts 5:1–5 (NIV)

The danger of deceit

Now a man named Ananias, together with his wife Sapphira, also sold a piece of property. With his wife's full knowledge he kept back part of the money for himself, but brought the rest and put it at the apostles' feet. Then Peter said. 'Ananias, how is it that Satan has so filled your heart that you have lied to the Holy Spirit and have kept for yourself some of the money you received for the land? Didn't it belong to you before it was sold? And after it was sold, wasn't the money at your disposal? What made you think of doing such a thing? You have not lied to men but to God.' When Ananias heard this he fell down and died. And great fear seized all who heard what had happened.

This dramatic story follows a passage that concentrates on the Christians' generosity with their possessions. Many of them sold property and entrusted the money to their leaders to use for the poor. Let's imagine Ananias and Sapphira talking together: *S.* People are asking why we haven't given away any of our lands. *A.* Aren't they ours to do with what we want? *S.* We could sell one of the fields and give part of the cash. *A.* And then pretend it was all we got from the sale.

How easily one suggestion leads to the next! In this story we see *The downward pull of human sin:* Greed and deceit characterize this couple. Peter recognized their right to ownership; his concern was their lies. *The reality of Satan:* When Ananias and Sapphira yielded to temptation they gave Satan an opportunity to enter their lives. Satan grabs any crack of human sin as an open door. Some people ignore his very existence; others blame him for everything that goes wrong. Both extremes are mistaken, but be warned of his activity. *The power of the Holy Spirit:* Jesus often knew what was in people's hearts. Peter, filled with the Spirit, had the same gift (which Paul calls a 'message of knowledge' in 1 Corinthians 12:8). God used it to convict Ananias of his sin.

A thought

Ananias was guilty; fear of God's judgment brought on his fatal heart attack. The church's fear was godly fear; that leads to repentance and change.

Acts 5:12–20 (NIV)

God's mighty power

The apostles performed many miraculous signs and wonders among the people. And all the believers used to meet together in Solomon's Colonnade. No-one else dared join them, even though they were highly regarded by the people. Nevertheless, more and more men and women believed in the Lord and were added to their number. As a result, people brought the sick into the streets . . . and all of them were healed. Then the high priest and all his associates . . . were filled with jealousy. They arrested the apostles and put them in the public jail. But during the night an angel of the Lord opened the doors of the jail and brought them out. 'Go, stand in the temple courts,' he said, 'and tell the people the full message of this new life.'

The Jewish leaders were determined to shut up the apostles—literally, in jail, and metaphorically, to keep them quiet. God had other ideas! *He exercised his power to heal.* We remember the crowds that thronged round Jesus. Power to heal did not end with Jesus—nor with the apostles. God still heals today, though such an intensive period of miracles is occasional, not all the time. *He continued to draw people to follow Jesus* through preaching and through miracles. *He sent an angel to free them from prison.* This, too, reminds me of Jesus in the gospels. 'An angel of the Lord came down from heaven and, going to the tomb, rolled back the stone' (Matthew 28:2). The power that freed Jesus is the same power that freed the apostles—and the same 'incomparably great power' is available 'for us who believe,' says Paul (Ephesians 1:19). *He emboldened them to keep preaching* despite the authorities' opposition.

A prayer

Father, I find it hard to believe these things can happen nowadays. To be honest, I'm scared. But I do want your Spirit to fill me, and to overflow in the way I live and the way I speak.

Acts 5:21–32 (NIV)

Unstoppable witnesses

At daybreak they entered the temple courts, as they had been told, and began to teach the people. When the high priest and his associates arrived, they called together the Sanhedrin—the full assembly of the elders of Israel—and sent to the jail for the apostles. But on arriving at the jail, the officers did not find them there . . . [They were found in the temple courts, teaching the people, and brought before the Sanhedrin and the High Priest.] 'We gave you strict orders not to teach in this name,' he said. 'Yet you have filled Jerusalem with your teaching and are determined to make us guilty of this man's blood.' Peter and the other apostles replied: 'We must obey God rather than men! The God of our fathers raised Jesus from the dead—whom you had killed by hanging him on a tree. God exalted him to his own right hand as Prince and Saviour that he might give repentance and forgiveness of sins to Israel. We are witnesses of these things and so is the Holy Spirit, whom God has given to those who obey him.'

Have you ever tried bobbing for apples? The buoyancy of the apple makes it almost impossible to hold down. The apostles were rather like that apple! However hard the Jewish authorities tried to check them from preaching they could not do it. Peter's words show us why they were so unsquashable. They were single-minded in their allegiance. 'We must obey God rather than men.' They knew it was God's power that 'raised Jesus from the dead' and 'exalted him to his own right hand.' They were witnesses. They had firsthand experience of Jesus' resurrection and ascension. They had been given the Holy Spirit.

A prayer

Lord God, I pray that I might know the hope to which you have called me, and the riches of your glorious inheritance in the saints, and your incomparably great power in us who believe: a power which is like the working of your mighty strength, which you exerted in Christ when you raised him from the dead and seated him at your right hand in the heavenly realms.

Based on Ephesians 1:17–23

Acts 5:33–39 (NIV)

Expediency and wisdom

When they heard this, they were furious and wanted to put them to death. But a Pharisee named Gamaliel, a teacher of the law, who was honoured by all the people, stood up in the Sanhedrin and ordered that the men be put outside for a little while. Then he addressed them: 'Men of Israel, consider carefully what you intend to do to these men. Some time ago Theudas appeared, claiming to be somebody, and about four hundred men rallied to him. He was killed, all his followers were dispersed, and it all came to nothing. After him, Judas the Galilean appeared in the days of the census and led a band of people in revolt. He too was killed, and all his followers were scattered. Therefore, in the present case I advise you: Leave these men alone! Let them go! For if their purpose or activity is of human origin, it will fail. But if it is from God, you will not be able to stop these men; you will only find yourselves fighting against God.'

The council members were understandably furious. They were the leaders and the experts on theological matters; they expected to be revered and obeyed. Now these uneducated followers of Jesus were accusing them of murder, constantly defying them, and attracting more and more followers through preaching apparent blasphemy! Killing them seemed the obvious way out. But among them was a wise, even-tempered man. Gamaliel knew that God was sovereign and that his good purposes would be worked out. Gamaliel's argument was simple. 'Wait and see what happens. If this is just a human revolt it will fade, as the others did. If it is of God'—as Gamaliel probably believed—'we do not want to be on the wrong side.' What wise words for precaution against panic reactions!

A way to pray

Meditate on those words of Gamaliel and ask yourself: Is God really in control? Can he be trusted one hundred per cent? What anxiety in my life now should I deliberately ask him to control?

John 15:1–5 (JB)

The sap of the Spirit

[Jesus said] 'I am the true vine, and my Father is the vinedresser. Every branch in me that bears no fruit he cuts away, and every branch that does bear fruit he prunes to make it bear even more. You are pruned already, by means of the word that I have spoken to you. Make your home in me, as I make mine in you. As a branch cannot bear fruit all by itself, but must remain part of the vine, neither can you unless you remain in me. I am the vine, you are the branches. Whoever remains in me, with me in him, bears fruit in plenty; for cut off from me you can do nothing.'

Last year I was walking through a vineyard in Cyprus on a hot autumn day. There was a cloudless blue sky over my head, the earth was a beautiful, rich red, and as I walked I listened to the sound of the sea. The grapes had been harvested, but the low vines were still covered with lush green leaves on their short, twisted branches. All except one branch. That was covered in dry, brown leaves, and torn off from the vine. It was dead, and when the farmer came to get the vineyard ready for next year he would throw it away and burn it. No hope of that branch bearing a rich crop of grapes next year. The life-giving sap of the vine couldn't get through to it.

Before the next harvest, though, all the branches in all the vines would be fiercely pruned. Then they would bear fruit. A lot of fruit. Beautiful bunches of sweet, juicy grapes carried on the twisted branches of the vine. Branches that on the outside look dead and dry. But inside them the rich, life-giving sap of the vine is flowing through, from the roots to the fruit. Like the Holy Spirit of God...

So reflect on the sap and the Spirit—and on the fact that it is the Father who prunes the branches... you and me... through all the circumstances and the pain of our lives... through what the world and other people do to us... and through what we do (and fail to do) to other people. There is always pain in the pruning—but God is always there in the pain with us.

SB

Acts 6:1–6 (NIV)

Spiritual administrators

In those days when the number of disciples was increasing, the Grecian Jews among them complained against the Hebraic Jews because their widows were being overlooked in the daily distribution of food. So the Twelve gathered all the disciples together and said, 'It would not be right for us to neglect the ministry of the word of God in order to wait on tables. Brothers, choose seven men from among you who are known to be full of the Spirit and wisdom. We will turn this responsibility over to them and will give our attention to prayer and the ministry of the word.' This proposal pleased the whole group. They chose Stephen, a man full of faith and of the Holy Spirit; also Philip, Procorus, Nicanor, Timon, Parmenas, and Nicolas from Antioch, a convert to Judaism. They presented these men to the apostles who prayed and laid their hands on them.

The apostles knew where their priorities lay, in prayer and preaching. But they were concerned for the good of the community and they were willing to delegate responsibility. It is noticeable that they did not make autocratic decisions but they consulted the whole congregation.

What qualities would you look for in those who were to be practical, caring administrators? Most of us would probably seek gifts of organization and social concern. What did the apostles look for? 'Men who are known to be full of the Spirit and wisdom.' That should be the prime aim of any of us who want to serve God in any capacity, whether in an upfront 'spiritual' ministry or in washing dishes, singing in the choir, as PCC members or sidespersons, in the church or in daily employment. We are prone to separate the 'sacred' from the 'secular', instead of submitting our lives to him as a whole. If we are 'full of the Spirit' we will consult him often during the day, whatever our occupation.

The names of the men chosen are all Greek names. Care was taken to choose those who would be trusted to be fair to everyone who had felt neglected. That shows wisdom.

A reflection

What lessons does this passage have for those who are church leaders? What encouragements for those who do the 'ordinary' jobs?

Acts 6:8–15 (NIV)

Christlikeness

Now Stephen, a man full of God's grace and power, did great wonders and miraculous signs among the people. Opposition arose, however, from members of the Synagogue of the Freedmen (as it was called)—Jews of Cyrene and Alexandria as well as the provinces of Cilicia and Asia. These men began to argue with Stephen, but they could not stand up against his wisdom or the Spirit by whom he spoke. Then they secretly persuaded some men to say, 'We have heard Stephen speak words of blasphemy against Moses and against God.' So they stirred up the people and the elders and the teachers of the law. They seized Stephen and brought him before the Sanhedrin. They produced false witnesses, who testified, 'This fellow never stops speaking against this holy place and against the law. For we have heard him say that this Jesus of Nazareth will destroy this place and change the customs Moses handed down to us.' All who were sitting in the Sanhedrin looked intently at Stephen, and they saw that his face was like the face of an angel.

Stephen was chosen by the congregation to serve food to the widows. He soon showed that he had gifts to use in other ways. As I read about Stephen I see in this Christian one who was very much a Christ-man. There are several remarkable similarities between Stephen and his master. If you can find time during the week, underline in your notes some of the phrases that remind you of Jesus.

Do you know anyone of whom you might say that his face, or her face, 'is like the face of an angel'? If we want to reflect the love and beauty of Jesus we start where Stephen started; he was 'full of the Spirit'. If we open ourselves to the Holy Spirit he will reveal Jesus to us and gradually make us more like our Master.

A reflection

Now the Lord is the Spirit, and where the Spirit of the Lord is, there is freedom. And we, who with unveiled faces all reflect [or contemplate] the Lord's glory, are being transformed into his likeness with ever-increasing glory, which comes from the Lord, who is the Spirit.

2 Corinthians 3:17,18 (NIV)

59

Acts 7:51–54 (NIV)

Angry blame

'You stiff-necked people, with uncircumcised hearts and ears! You are just like your fathers: You always resist the Holy Spirit! Was there ever a prophet your fathers did not persecute? They even killed those who predicted the coming of the Righteous One. And now you have betrayed and murdered him—you who have received the law that was put into effect through angels but have not obeyed it.' When they heard this, they were furious and gnashed their teeth at him.

Stephen was accused by false witnesses of speaking against the temple, the law and their customs. So the high priest asked him whether these complaints were true. His reply took his hearers through the early history of their own nation, from Abraham's call to leave Mesopotamia through to Solomon building the temple. His theme was the repeated misunderstanding and rejection received by Joseph, Moses and others. His hearers listened patiently; Stephen clearly knew his ancient history. So long as he was speaking about others they were not touched; but as soon as he confronted them directly they were convicted—and they were furious.

It is easy to point a finger at other people. But a hand that points a forefinger at another has three other fingers pointing back at the person doing the pointing. 'If any of you is without sin, let him be the first to throw a stone at her,' said Jesus to those who brought him a woman accused of adultery. Honesty made them gradually disappear. When we see that we are as much to blame as others we can react in two ways. We can turn our guilt into anger, as these men did against Stephen. Or our guilt can lead us to confession, repentance and finding God's forgiveness.

A confession

Before you use this confession, read it through. Then stop and think honestly how it applies to you, so that you can be specific and genuine in your prayer.
Lord, I think of the times when I have blamed others when I was guilty myself. Please forgive me for my unfairness, especially when others have been hurt by it. Show me where I should apologize or make restitution.

Acts 7:55–8:1 (NIV)

A Christlike death

But Stephen, full of the Holy Spirit, looked up to heaven and saw the glory of God, and Jesus standing at the right hand of God. 'Look,' he said, 'I see heaven open and the Son of Man standing at the right hand of God.' At this they covered their ears and, yelling at the top of their voices, they all rushed at him, dragged him out of the city and began to stone him. Meanwhile, the witnesses laid their clothes at the feet of a young man named Saul. While they were stoning him, Stephen prayed, 'Lord Jesus, receive my spirit.' Then he fell on his knees and cried out, 'Lord, do not hold this sin against them.' When he had said this, he fell asleep. And Saul was there, giving approval to his death.

Stephen was filled with the Holy Spirit. The Spirit gave him a rare experience, a vision of the majesty and glory of God and of the Son of Man (an Old Testament name for the Messiah). His death, like that of Jesus, was ugly and cruel. Yet through the Spirit he behaved like Jesus, forgiving those who hurt him and entrusting his spirit to God. It is the same Spirit who can transform our own prayer and worship, to help us sense the glory of the almighty God. It is the Spirit who helps us to forgive those who wrong us and to trust our whole lives to him.

The members of the Sanhedrin were shaken by the events of recent months. But they were sincerely convinced that Stephen was blaspheming in his claim to see God; so they were obeying the Jewish law in stoning him—no doubt delighted to have the final excuse for their anger to boil over in killing him. It is possible to be sincere but utterly wrong—especially when our emotions want to convince us that we are right. Saul only played a small part in this event, but Luke's mention of his presence implies that it made a significant impact on him and played a part in his subsequent conversion.

A way to pray
Look back at the Bible readings for the last three days. In what ways would you like to be like Stephen? Then, in prayer, open yourself to God to change you.

Psalm 71:14–19 (BCP)

Full stature

I will go forth in the strength of the Lord God: and will make mention of thy righteousness only. Thou, O God, hast taught me from my youth up until now: therefore will I tell of thy wondrous works. Forsake me not, O God, in mine old age, when I am gray-headed: until I have shewed thy strength unto this generation, and thy power to all them that are yet for to come. Thy righteousness, O God, is very high: and great things are they that thou hast done; O God, who is like unto thee? O what great troubles and adversities hast thou shewed me! and yet didst thou turn and refresh me: yea, and broughtest me from the deep of the earth again. Thou hast brought me to great honour: and comforted me on every side.

Some biblical texts seem to belong to us as individuals. We say, 'Ah, that is my verse. I love that one.' The first verse in today's reading is a bit like that for me. I was sitting in Fulham Palace Chapel on the eve of my ordination. I was nervous. I did not know what lay ahead. Would I be able to fulfil this ministry? Then the Bishop of London swept into the Chapel, arrayed in purple. Standing there he said to us all, 'This is the verse for each one of you: "I will go forth in the strength of the Lord God and will make mention of thy righteousness only."'

This psalm comes into its own when we have reached middle age and can look back and also begin wondering about the future. God has been with us all the way. We felt very small when we began but in middle life we seem to have achieved something. We are at our best when we reach our full stature. The past has made us what we are under God. But what about the declining years? The Psalmist worried a bit, hence the prayer earlier in the psalm: 'Cast me not away in the time of age: forsake me not when my strength faileth me' (v. 8).

A prayer

Lord, you have never let me go and never will. I will go forth still in your strength.

DCF

Psalm 19:1–3,7,8,13–14 (RSV)

Clean living

The heavens are telling the glory of God; and the firmament proclaims his handiwork. Day to day pours forth speech, and night to night declares knowledge. There is no speech, nor are there words; their voice is not heard; yet their voice goes out through all the earth, and their words to the end of the world . . . The law of the Lord is perfect, reviving the soul; the testimony of the Lord is sure, making wise the simple . . . the fear of the Lord is clean, enduring for ever . . . Keep back thy servant also from presumptuous sins; let them not have dominion over me . . . Let the words of my mouth and the meditation of my heart be acceptable in thy sight, O Lord, my rock and my redeemer.

Psalm 19 is said to be the finest in the Psalter and one of the greatest lyrics in the world. I am not competent to make such a literary judgment but I felt I had to include this psalm in my collection for comment.

It is divided into three parts. First the Psalmist speaks of the world of nature, then of the law and finally a personal prayer to safeguard us from pomposity and priggishness. He starts with the sky and in particular the sun, its daily triumphant procession from East to West, and especially its heat beating down as it does in the Eastern Mediterranean lands into every nook and cranny. It tells of the power of the Creator.

Then the Psalmist speaks of the law summarised in the ten commandments. Like the sun it probes into all the shady parts of our lives, and we try to hide from it. But it is sanitary, disinfectant, cleansing. Life conducted in a way that blocks it out breeds disease. The Hebrews looking out on the nations bordering their land were aghast at the cruelty and filth. In the twentieth century we have seen this kind of degradation take over where the Christian ethics have been thrown out either in hostility or in ridicule. But we must pray for deliverance from self righteousness. The Psalmist knows this. See how his poem ends.

A prayer

Lord, keep your Church in the way of your commandment, whatever the opposition, whatever the ridicule: but with humility and grace.

DCF

Romans 6:3–4 (NEB)

Called to life

Have you forgotten that when we were baptized into union with Christ Jesus we were baptized into his death? By baptism we were buried with him, and lay dead, in order that, as Christ was raised from the dead in the splendour of the Father, so also we might set our feet upon the new path of life.

Today, all over the world, people are being baptized. Some will be adults, and some will be children. Some will believe that baptism automatically makes the baptized person a Christian, others will see it as done in hope, others as an act of faith and witness. But whatever our view of baptism, this passage makes it clear that one important part of our baptism is that it is a call.

It is a call to live a new life through faith in Christ. Today, look back at your baptism. It doesn't matter whether you remember the event or not; what counts here is that you have been baptized. That baptism was God's call to serve him and live for him.

The imagery of death and burial in baptism is a call to take action to put to death the parts of our lives that cannot exist in the presence of Christ; the petty sins and selfishness, the worries and fears that point to our weakness of faith. These are part of the old life which in Christ we are called to leave behind.

When we take part in Holy Communion, we again stress the idea of dying. As Jesus died for us, so we share in the benefits of his death, and respond to the call of baptism by receiving God's strength to enable us to put our old selves to death.

Baptism and Communion both set us the pattern of Christian life; the pattern of dying and rising, of leaving behind the old and setting out with the new. So today, respond to the call of baptism and the grace of communion, and offer yourself afresh to God, to live for him.

MM

The Story of Elijah

This month we are going to read the story of Elijah, from 1 and 2 Kings. Stories play an important part in our lives—we tell them for entertainment and for teaching, to inspire, frighten or provoke thought.

The Bible is full of stories, in both the Old and New Testaments, yet we so rarely read them as stories, at least once we are out of Sunday School. Instead, we try to treat them as doctrinal statements, or spiritual meditations. Of course, they do contribute to our understanding of the faith, and they do build up our spiritual experience, but they do it by acting as stories, not as textbooks.

So this month, we shall not bother with questions of who wrote the story (or, more probably, first told it) or how historical it is. (Some stories are 'true' and others are 'fiction' and many others are neither or both.) We shall simply read through most of the story and ask ourselves questions along the way. We may have to miss one or two bits out, so it may be a good idea to sit down for half an hour with your Bible and read the whole story through.

As you read it, you will find yourself asking questions of your own. They may be the ones we shall ask together in these notes, but that's unlikely, so between us, we ought to gain quite a lot from the story of Elijah.

When we read stories, we always read them from our own particular viewpoint. The way we read Elijah's story will be very different from the way its first hearers heard it, for we shall approach it as Christians, knowing far more of what happens later. But that is all right, because all the stories of the Bible are linked by the one most important character: God. All stories are, in a way, his story.

Marcus Maxwell

1 Kings 16:29–33 (REB)

The villain

Ahab the son of Omri became king of Israel in the thirty-eighth year of King Asa of Judah, and he reigned over Israel in Samaria for twenty-two years. More than any of his predecessors, he did what was wrong in the eyes of the Lord. As if it were not enough for him to follow the sinful ways of Jeroboam son of Nebat, he took as his wife Jezebel daughter of King Ethbaal of Sidon, and went and served Baal; he prostrated himself before him and erected an altar to him in the temple of Baal which he built in Samaria. He also set up a sacred pole; indeed, he did more to provoke the anger of the Lord the God of Israel than all the kings of Israel before him.

My five-year-old son is happy to listen to any story or watch any TV programme, as long as he is sure who are the goodies and the baddies. In the story of Elijah, it is clear from the outset who is the baddie. It is King Ahab, aided by his foreign queen, Jezebel! Of course, Ahab didn't see it that way. By marrying the king of Sidon's daughter, he had made a powerful alliance with a nation which was at the centre of civilization. In those days, treaties were sealed by oaths to the gods of both sides. An altar to Baal Melkart of Sidon was hardly too great a price for the hope of prosperity. And it was only fair to allow Jezebel the freedom to practise her own religion, to bring a few priests and prophets of her own god. It seemed a harmless compromise. But there were dangers. The people of Israel were always tempted to hedge their bets by acknowledging the gods of the local nations—after all, they were local gods and should be pretty effective. Also, Israel's kings were responsible to their people and to God. The surrounding kings were absolute despots, who would see Ahab's concern to please his people as weakness. Ahab would have to show greater strength if he was to remain credible.

It was a small compromise, for great benefits. Yet it carried the seeds of disaster for Israel, for it was a denial of God's demand for exclusive loyalty to him.

A question

How are you tempted to compromise between your loyalty to God and fitting in with the world around?

1 Kings 17:1–6 (REB)

Opposition

Elijah the Tishbite from Tishbe in Gilead said to Ahab, 'I swear by the life of the Lord the God of Israel, whose servant I am, that there will be neither dew nor rain these coming years unless I give the word.' Then the word of the Lord came to him, 'Leave this place, turn eastwards, and go into hiding in the wadi of Kerith east of the Jordan. You are to drink from the stream, and I have commanded the ravens to feed you there.' Elijah did as the Lord had told him: he went and stayed in the wadi of Kerith east of the Jordan, and the ravens brought him bread and meat morning and evening, and he drank from the stream.

Who was Elijah? We are told where he came from, but nothing more. Was he from one of the travelling bands of prophets who wandered the countryside? Had he been attached to a shrine? Who were his parents, his teachers, his friends? We don't know. He appears in the story like the mysterious stranger who rides into town, and who we know will sort out the bad guys in the end.

But we don't need to know much about Elijah. His qualifications aren't what count. What really matters is that he is God's man, and he is here when he is needed.

I remember when a new minister arrived in a church I used to attend. He turned things upside-down, and his preaching challenged and shattered what had become a cosy club. 'Who does he think he is?' someone asked. 'What authority does he have?' In fact, he had the only authority he really needed—he was faithful to God in a time and a place when faithfulness was at a premium. He became God's man for that church, and great things began to happen.

So Elijah appears on the scene and confronts Ahab. He may be a lone voice, but he is faithful to God, and God's power is with him.

A reflection

Who is God's person where you are? Who is faithful to him? Is it you? Or should it be?

1 Kings 17:7–10 (NEB)

The nameless widow

After a while, the stream dried up, for there had been no rain in the land. Then the word of the Lord came to him: 'Go now to Zarephath, a village of Sidon, and stay there; I have commanded a widow there to feed you.' He went off to Zarephath, and when he reached the entrance to the village, he saw a widow gathering sticks.

Elijah stays with the widow of Zarephath for going on three years, yet we are never told her name. Some feminist readers might say this is because, as a woman, she is not important for the male dominated society in which she lived, and in which the story was first told. There is some truth in that. As a single woman, her place was hardly worthy of notice. She had no man to defend her, provide for her or give her status in society. Yet God sent his prophet to her to be cared for and hidden from Ahab.

Or again, perhaps it's her social position which makes her forgettable. Without a male provider, a widow was the poorest of the poor—when Elijah arrives, she is preparing for death by starvation. She was one of the forgotten people, overlooked by family (if she had any) and neighbours. Thrown on life's scrap-heap she meant nothing to anyone. Yet God sent Elijah to her.

Perhaps, though, it's because she was a Gentile. One of the people of Jezebel's country of Sidon. Not one of the chosen of Israel, but an outsider, worshipping false gods. Hardly one of the great heroes of the Bible. Yet, again, it is to her that Elijah is sent by God.

Whatever the reason, her lack of a name in the story seems to show that she is a 'non-person', of no significance. Yet the story itself undermines that view, for she is the one God has commanded to look after Elijah. So what do we make of this insignificant person who is so significant?

Simply this: God finds her significant, no matter what other people may think. In a story that deals with the sins of kings, the wars of nations and the clash of prophets, an ordinary, insignificant person takes, for a time, the centre stage, and because of her, God's story can continue.

A prayer

Thank you Father, that I matter. Not because I am rich, or powerful or gifted, but because I matter to you.

1 Kings 17:10–15 (REB)

Never-ending story

He went off to Zarephath, and when he reached the entrance to the village, he saw a widow gathering sticks. He called to her, 'Please bring me a little water in a pitcher to drink.' As she went to fetch it, he called after her, 'Bring me, please, a piece of bread as well.' But she answered, 'As the Lord your God lives, I have no food baked, only a handful of flour in a jar and a little oil in a flask. I am just gathering two or three sticks to go and cook it for my son and myself before we die.' 'Have no fear,' said Elijah; 'go and do as you have said. But first make a small cake from what you have and bring it out to me, and after that make something for your son and yourself. For this is the word of the Lord the God of Israel: The jar of flour will not give out, nor the flask of oil fail, until the Lord sends rain on the land.' She went and did as Elijah had said, and there was food for him and for her and her family for a long time.

It is hard not to see an echo of the story of Jesus and the loaves and fishes which fed a multitude (or perhaps it is the other way round). And that is not strange, for all the Bible's stories are part of the one Story, the tale of salvation. From Genesis to Revelation, the story of God and his people is told, and we are in the midst of that story.

So here, and in the Gospels, and in our own lives, God takes the little we have to offer and uses it for his own purposes. With God, it is always enough.

In my own church, there is a woman who claims that she really has very little to offer for her work with the children's teaching ministry.

Perhaps she is right—but she gets on very well. Because she is part of this story.

A reflection

It isn't what you have to offer to God that counts, but whether you offer it.

1 Kings 17:17–22 (REB)

Breath of life

Afterwards, the son of the woman, the owner of the house, fell ill and was in a very bad way, until at last his breathing stopped. The woman said to Elijah, 'What made you interfere, you man of God? You came here to bring my sins to light and cause my son's death!' 'Give me your son,' he said. He took the boy from her arms and carried him up to the roof-chamber where his lodging was, and laid him on the bed. He called out to the Lord, 'Lord my God, is this your care for the widow with whom I lodge, that you have been so cruel to her son?' Then he breathed deeply on the child three times, and called to the Lord, 'I pray, Lord my God, let the breath of life return to the body of this child.' The Lord listened to Elijah's cry, and the breath of life returned to the child's body, and he revived.

What is the key word in this story? Surely it is 'breath'. The boy doesn't simply 'die'—his breathing stops. It is his breath that Elijah uses to symbolize life, and returning breath that he prays for.

Breath is a major theme in the Bible, and all the more so when we remember that the words for breath and soul, wind and spirit are all related. In Genesis, God forms the first human from the soil, and *breathes* life into him.

Life is the gift of God, and not only physical life, but spiritual life. Elijah is a prophet, full of the Spirit/breath of God, and from that Spirit, new breath returns to the dead child.

In the Christian story, it is the Spirit of God who comes to bring new life, and by the breath of God we are born again. The new life that Jesus offers is life brought to us by the Holy Spirit who dwells in our hearts.

A way to pray
Turn your breathing into prayer. Concentrate on the flow of air into you, and make it a prayer that the Spirit of God will flow into all your life as the air brings life to every cell of your body.

1 Kings 17:23–24 (REB)

Up and down faith

Elijah lifted him and took him down from the roof-chamber into the house, and giving him to his mother he said, 'Look, your son is alive.' She said to Elijah, 'Now I know for certain that you are a man of God and that the word of the Lord on your lips is truth.'

Well, we might say, she ought to have got the idea from the way the flour and oil were still going strong. And of course, she did. The nameless widow knew Elijah was God's man, but as with all of us, her attitude to God swung wildly. No doubt she was thankful and awed by the miraculous supply of food. Then she was angry and guilty over her son's illness and death ('It's all my fault; God is punishing me for my sins'). Then she was overjoyed by his marvellous recovery.

In fact, what we take to be our spiritual state is more often due to our physical or emotional condition. We can probably all identify with the changes in the woman's attitude. Not long ago, I was afraid I was developing a serious illness. I prayed frantically, and rather bitterly and whiningly, but God seemed very far away. Then I was pronounced all clear (for now at least!) and I was ready to sing God's praises with all the company of heaven.

I don't really think I was any closer to God at any particular point of my ups and downs, but my normal human reactions told me otherwise. The point is that what I felt was normal and natural, as were the widow's various reactions. In our spiritual life, we need to take notice of our bodies and minds, and to be aware of the part they play in our prayer and feelings.

None of these feelings and attitudes is wrong, but they are a part of who we are, the person God created. Too often we try to separate our faith from the rest of us, and it simply can't be done.

A way to pray

Spend some time reflecting on your present situation; health, finances, family or whatever. How do they affect the way you feel? Make those feelings the basis of your prayer, as you offer them to God.

Deuteronomy 7:6–9a (NEB)

Grace

You are a people holy to the Lord your God; the Lord your God chose you out of all nations on earth to be his special possession. It was not because you were more numerous than any other nation that the Lord cared for you and chose you, for you were the smallest of all nations; it was because the Lord loved you and stood by his oath to your forefathers, that he brought you out with his strong hand and redeemed you from the land of slavery, from the power of Pharaoh king of Egypt. Know then that the Lord your God is God, the faithful God . . .

One of the saddest things about many Christians is the way their faith is tinged with guilt. 'I know I ought to pray more . . .' 'I really ought to go to church more often . . .' 'I wish I was a better person . . .' Sometimes what we feel bad about is genuinely wrong. At other times it is imaginary. But whether the faults we lament are real or not, our guilt is based on a false idea of God.

In today's reading, Moses tells the Israelites that there is nothing special about them—except for the one important thing, that they belong to God. And they belong to God because he loved them and kept his promises, no matter what they were like.

We could do with remembering this. When we become aware of our faults and begin to feel guilty, we need to remember that God loves us. That is, he loves *us*—not some ideal of what we ought to be, but the real us, faults and all. He has chosen us, not because we are good, but simply out of love.

When we grasp that, our prayers and our worship are liberated from the feeling that we ought to try harder to please him, and instead become a joyful celebration, not of our worth, but his gracious love. Today in your prayers, forget what you are like, and think only of what God is like—unconditionally loving.

MM

1 Kings 18:1–6 (REB)

Secret hero

Time went by, and in the third year the word of the Lord came to Elijah: 'Go, appear before Ahab, and I shall send rain on the land.' So Elijah went to show himself to Ahab. At this time the famine in Samaria was at its height, and Ahab summoned Obadiah, the comptroller of his household, a devout worshipper of the Lord. When Jezebel massacred the prophets of the Lord, he had taken a hundred of them, hidden them in caves, fifty by fifty, and sustained them with food and drink. Ahab said to Obadiah, 'Let us go throughout the land to every spring and wadi; if we can find enough grass we may keep the horses and mules alive and not lose any of our animals.' They divided the land between them for their survey, Ahab himself going one way, and Obadiah another.

'The blood of the martyrs,' wrote the church Father, Irenaeus, 'is the seed of the church.' And so it is. Those whose faithfulness to God stands firm up to the point of death are a witness (martyros in Greek) to the Lordship of Christ and his claim to our first obedience. But martyrdom is a gift of God which is not given to everyone. In times of persecution, there are always those who stand by their faith quietly and in an unspectacular way work for God.

One such person was Obadiah. A high official in Ahab's government, he remained faithful to the Lord of Israel and was able to use his power to save the lives of many of the prophets who were threatened by the queen's zeal for her god.

Again we see a minor character in the story who yet has an important role. And he is a reminder (as God will later remind Elijah) that true faith can never be stamped out—try as they will, the forces of evil will never extinguish it. One of the most moving news items I have ever seen was a picture of a priest in Romania celebrating Mass in a city square on Christmas Eve after the end of communism. A crowd of thousands heard for the first time the meaning of Christmas.

So pray for those of your fellow Christians who hold the faith quietly and in adversity, treasuring the flame against the time when once again it will burn brightly.

1 Kings 18:7–12,15,16 (REB)

Unpleasant tasks

As Obadiah went on his way, Elijah suddenly confronted him. Obadiah recognized Elijah and prostrated himself before him. 'Can it really be you, my lord Elijah?' he said. 'Yes,' he replied, 'it is I. Go and tell your master that Elijah is here.' 'What wrong have I done?' protested Obadiah. 'Why should you give me into Ahab's hands? He will put me to death. As the Lord your God lives, there is no region or kingdom to which my master has not sent in search of you. If they said, "He is not here," he made that kingdom or region swear an oath that you could not be found. Yet now you say, "Go and tell your master that Elijah is here." What will happen? As soon as I leave you, the spirit of the Lord will carry you away, who knows where? I shall go and tell Ahab, and when he fails to find you he will kill me . . .' Elijah answered, 'As the Lord of Hosts lives, whose servant I am, I swear that I shall show myself to him this day.' So Obadiah went to find Ahab and gave him the message, and Ahab went to confront Elijah.

It has been said that the reward for doing a difficult task is to be set a harder one. After a life of faithful and often dangerous service, Obadiah finds himself confronted with an apparent command to commit suicide.

If we think for a few moments we can probably sympathize. Do you remember that time when you really believed that you should do something that was right, that was God's will, but it filled you with fear?

We know too, that Jesus himself faced the same fear—knowing God's will, but seeing the task as too great for human courage. Yet Jesus knew that God was to be trusted. Obadiah was to find that, too. And so must we. God doesn't set us tasks without giving us the power to see them through.

A reflection

Is there any task you face which seems too much? Is it the right thing to do? Then thank God for the strength he has ready for you, and trust him for it.

1 Kings 18:17–20 (NEB)

Different viewpoints

As soon as Ahab saw Elijah, he said to him, 'Is it you, you troubler of Israel?' 'It is not I who have brought trouble on Israel,' Elijah replied, 'but you and your father's family, by forsaking the commandments of the Lord and following Baal. Now summon all Israel to meet me on Mount Carmel, including the four hundred and fifty prophets of Baal and the four hundred prophets of the goddess Asherah, who are attached to Jezebel's household.' So Ahab sent throughout the length and breadth of Israel and assembled the prophets on Mount Carmel.

Perhaps it's fanciful, but I feel I can detect a certain respect between Ahab and Elijah. Ahab knows (though he will not admit it) that Elijah is indeed a prophet of the God of Israel- –though that God is troublesome and prone not to keep in his proper place; not at all like the more convenient gods of his neighbours. Elijah knows that Ahab is still the king of God's people, and for that reason not entirely abandoned by God.

Each sees the other as the cause of Israel's problems. The troublesome prophet of a troublesome God, interfering in politics and economics and all kinds of non-religious affairs faces the worldly-wise king, leading his people into strong alliances and economic prosperity, and away from God. Perhaps they should just agree to differ, live and let live, and let people choose their own religion and their own lifestyle?

But that won't do. Elijah knows that in the end there is no middle ground, no balancing of options. There is God or nothing.

A reflection

What do you try to balance out with God? What other things do you give equal weight to, or try to keep separate from the life of faith? How successful are you?

1 Kings 18:21–24 (REB)

Moment of truth

Elijah stepped forward towards all the people there and said, 'How long will you sit on the fence? If the Lord is God, follow him; but if Baal, then follow him.' Not a word did they answer. Then Elijah said, 'I am the only prophet of the Lord still left, but there are four hundred and fifty prophets of Baal. Bring two bulls for us. Let them choose one for themselves, cut it up, and lay it on the wood without setting fire to it, and I shall prepare the other and lay it on the wood without setting fire to it. Then invoke your god by name and I shall invoke the Lord by name; the god who answers by fire, he is God.' The people all shouted their approval.

Well, they would, wouldn't they? What a spectacle; and no admission fee! But how many realized what Elijah was truly saying? Today the people of Israel faced a great choice. It was the choice that Moses had put to their ancestors, and Joshua after him: 'Choose today whom you will serve.'

Like their king they were sitting on the fence. Not exactly denying God, but allowing themselves plenty of room for other options. But they had to make up their minds. There could be no half measures with God.

What Elijah was offering was not truly a once for all choice. It was a commitment to a life of choice. Each day we are faced with hundreds of choices, and in many of them God has a part to play. We choose afresh each day whether to serve God. On waking, as we commit the day to him (or not), as we meet people who annoy us and we respond in love and forgive-

ness (or not), as we give precious time to friends and family (or not), as we accept opportunities to do good (or not).

We often fail to make the right choice. But there is good news in our story too—God had given the choice to Israel before, but he was still willing to come back and offer it again. In the grace of God, failure is never final, as long as we are willing to make the right choice again.

A way to pray
Offer to God your choices and ask for his guidance. Offer your failures and ask him for his forgiveness.

1 Kings 18:25–40 (parts) (NEB)

Triumph

Elijah said to the prophets of Baal, 'Choose one of the bulls and offer it first, for there are more of you; invoke your god by name, but do not set fire to the wood.' . . .and they invoked Baal by name from morning until noon, crying, 'Baal, answer us'; but there was no sound, no answer . . . At midday Elijah mocked them: 'Call louder, for he is a god. It may be he is in deep thought, or engaged, or on a journey . . .' All afternoon they raved and ranted till the time of the regular offering, but still there was no sound, no answer, no sign of attention . . . At the hour of the regular offering, the prophet Elijah came forward and prayed . . . The fire of the Lord fell, consuming the whole-offering, the wood, the stones, and the earth, and licking up the water in the trench. At the sight, the people all bowed with their faces to the ground and cried, 'The Lord is God, the Lord is God.' They [the prophets of Baal] were seized, and Elijah took them down to the Kishon and slaughtered them there in the valley.

The power of God is demonstrated without a doubt. Even soaked and surrounded with water, the sacrifice is ignited, and the people rise up and do away with the prophets of the false god. A terrible and bloody triumph, but one which is bound to restore Israel to the right path. The drought is ended, as God pours rain and blessing on his people.

It seems the perfect ending. The wicked witch is dead, the hero is victorious, and the people live happily ever after. If only life were really like that. But we know that our moments of joy and triumph are undermined by the future. The story for us goes on, and there will be sorrow and failure ahead.

Wait a bit, though. Elijah's story isn't over either. There is sorrow and failure for him too. But that can't remove the fact of this victory. Perhaps we could learn from him that moments of glory are the gift of God and should be thankfully received. We know that our moments of joy and wonder are not for ever, but don't let that detract from what we receive.

A way to pray

Think of your times of wonder and triumph, and give thanks for them.

1 Kings 19:1–5 (REB)

Despair

When Ahab told Jezebel all that Elijah had done and how he had put all the prophets to the sword, she sent this message to Elijah, 'The gods do the same to me and more, unless by this time tomorrow I have taken your life as you took theirs.' In fear he fled for his life, and when he reached Beersheba in Judah he left his servant there, while he himself went a day's journey into the wilderness. He came to a broom bush, and sitting under it he prayed for death: 'It is enough,' he said, 'now, Lord, take away my life, for I am no better than my fathers before me.'

It should have been so different. The people should have demanded a return to the old ways of God. Ahab, surely convinced by the miracle of Carmel, should have sent Jezebel home and broken off the alliance she represented. The great event should have sparked renewal in Israel. Instead, the queen was firmly in charge of Ahab and Israel, and out for blood. Surely evil was triumphant.

Part of the problem was no doubt the Israelites. They had had their revival meeting and seen great wonders. But now they were back on their farms and life seemed much the same as usual. Elijah too was back to earth with a bump. Religious fervour is so hard to sustain.

Perhaps we also know the feeling. God is so close, the power of his Spirit almost tangible. We can do anything. (Elijah ran for miles ahead of Ahab's chariot.) Then it all fades, and we doubt even the memory.

But as we saw yesterday, the great events are special gifts. The real business of knowing God is about everyday life. We are not made for a continual high (at least not in this life). We are made to serve God in the everyday business of his world, and the real test of faith is not the frequency of great spiritual experiences but the continual working out of our relationship with God. And when we get that right, there is joy of a different kind.

A way to pray

Look at the day ahead of you and what you know you will be doing. Offer each activity to God in advance.

Exodus 20:1–4 (NEB)

Uncontrollable God

God spoke, and these were his words: I am the Lord your God who brought you out of Egypt, out of the land of slavery. You shall have no other god to set against me. You shall not make a carved image for yourself nor the likeness of anything in the heavens above, or on the earth below, or in the waters under the earth.

When I was a student, an Old Testament lecturer commented that many of the prophets really didn't understand the idolatry they condemned. They laughed at other nations for worshipping gods of stone and wood, but no one really believed that the idol was the god—it was a focus for the presence of the god and an aid to worship. Looked at in that light, the commandment against idols seems a bit extreme.

But I think the prophets understood idolatry all too well. Of course the idol wasn't thought to be the god. But that isn't the point. An idol gave an idea of what the god was like, and brought it down to human scale. It gave a sense of control over the god. And the true God cannot be limited by human imagination. The commandment against idolatry is saying, 'Don't think you can control God; he alone knows what he is like.' Or as he put it to Moses, 'I am who I am.' Not what we like to think he is.

Yet in time, God did provide an image of himself. Not a model or statue, but a living human being, in whom we see God: Jesus Christ.

When we pray, we are to pray not to the God we imagine, or the God we would like to have, but to the real God. And, thank God, we have an image we can grasp, yet which still stretches our understanding, as we pray to the Father through his Son.

MM

1 Kings 19:5–9 (REB)

Help on the way

[Elijah] lay down under the bush and, while he slept, an angel touched him and said, 'Rise and eat.' He looked, and there at his head was a cake baked on hot stones, and a pitcher of water. He ate and drank and lay down again. The angel of the Lord came again and touched him a second time, saying, 'Rise and eat; the journey is too much for you.' He rose and ate and drank and, sustained by this food, he went on for forty days and forty nights to Horeb, the mount of God. There he entered a cave where he spent the night.

The picture of Elijah's exhaustion (emotional and spiritual as well as physical) is as realistic as that of his despair. He slumps at the end of his tether, and rises only to take food before collapsing again. Even the marvellous provider of the food is not enough to excite a spark of interest.

Elijah's story is not one of high-flying spirituality. Like ours, it is a tale with its own share of weariness and defeat. But along the way, Elijah receives help; unexpected and miraculous—and nothing like enough.

Or at least, so it might have seemed to him. What he would have needed was surely a full return to strength, and the assurance that he would triumph in the end. But what he gets is a couple of meals and a long walk. In the end though, it turns out to be enough after all.

Time and again we discover that God is not the instant cure for all our problems. In grief or sorrow, anguish or despair, we call to him—and the final all-satisfying answer to our troubles fails to appear. What does come, however, is the strength or the courage or the determination to take a few more steps through our troubles, until at last, like Elijah, we pass through them.

The simple fact is that though our road may often seem weary, it is generally the only one we can follow to reach the point that God is taking us to. Along the way we get his help. It is often not the help we could wish for, but it is always what we need.

A reflection
'My grace is sufficient for you.'
2 Corinthians 12:9 (RSV)

1 Kings 19:9b–13 (REB)

Restoration

The word of the Lord came to him: 'Why are you here, Elijah?' 'Because of my great zeal for the Lord, the God of Hosts,' he replied. 'The people of Israel have forsaken your covenant, torn down your altars, and put your prophets to the sword. I alone am left, and they seek to take my life.' To this the answer came: 'Go and stand on the mount before the Lord.' The Lord was passing by: a great and strong wind came, rending mountains and shattering rocks before him, but the Lord was not in the wind; and after the wind there was an earthquake, but the Lord was not in the earthquake; and after the earthquake fire, but the Lord was not in the fire; and after the fire a faint murmuring sound. When Elijah heard it, he wrapped his face in his cloak and went and stood in the entrance to the cave. There came a voice: 'Why are you here, Elijah?'

Elijah can only repeat his earlier words. He is here because he has been faithful to God—and see what a mess that has got him into! It is a cry of self-pity, and a cry of doubt. If God is so great, if God has called Elijah to be his prophet, if God has shown himself able to work marvels, then why is everything coming apart?

God's answer is simple, and tomorrow we shall see it. For now, it is more important simply to see what Elijah is doing. He is complaining to God. There is a great tradition in the Bible of complaint to God, and we need to take it seriously. At the simplest level it is better to scream and shout at God than to ignore him or give up on him.

We get a flavour of this in Jesus' Gethsemane prayer, where anguish almost leads to rebellion against God's will. But the important thing is to keep the channel of communication open. As long as we do that, God will respond.

A way to pray

Bring out into the open all your doubts and fears; the thoughts that you are ashamed to admit are there, the questioning of God's love and goodness, his power and compassion. Lay them before God—but don't expect a clearer answer than Elijah (or Jesus) got.

1 Kings 19:15–18 (REB)

Faith

The Lord said to him, 'Go back by way of the wilderness of Damascus, enter the city, and anoint Hazael to be king of Aram; anoint also Jehu son of Nimshi to be king of Israel, and Elisha son of Shaphat of Abel-meholah to be prophet in your place. Whoever escapes the sword of Hazael Jehu will slay, and whoever escapes the sword of Jehu Elisha will slay. But I shall leave seven thousand in Israel, all who have not bowed the knee to Baal, all whose lips have not kissed him.'

Elijah has come, after a long journey, to the place where God made his covenant with the people of Israel. On the way, he has been supported by God, and here he has poured out his grief and despair. Surely, now that God has met him to his face, he will find out the answer to his fears and desperation?

At first sight, it seems not. All that happens is that he is given a list of new jobs to do. But with them comes a promise—that God is in charge, and that the new tasks will lead to a revolution in Israel which will put the nation back on God's path.

For Elijah and us there are several lessons here. Firstly, Elijah is not alone; there are seven thousand Israelites (no small number in those days) who are still faithful to God. It is Elijah's pride which has led him to think that he is alone, and that he is the only one that God can depend on.

With that news comes the further revelation that Elijah's task will not end in his lifetime. Just as we are part of the one great story, so is Elijah. His work is only a part of the whole work of God, and it will go on far beyond his death.

But by far the greatest news is that though everything has seemed pointless, God is working out his plan. He knows what will come of Elijah's work (and ours). Our part is to trust him and carry on with the job we have been given.

A prayer

Thank you, Father, that you are in charge. When things seem hopeless to me, remind me that you know what you are doing, and give me the grace to carry on with the task that is my part of the whole story.

1 Kings 19:19–21 (REB)

True owner

Elijah departed and found Elisha son of Shaphat ploughing; there were twelve pair of oxen ahead of him, and he himself was with the last of them. As Elijah passed, he threw his cloak over him. Elisha, leaving his oxen, ran after Elijah and said, 'Let me kiss my father and mother goodbye, and then I shall follow you.' 'Go back,' he replied, 'what have I done to prevent you?' He followed him no farther but went home, took his pair of oxen, slaughtered them, and burnt the wooden yokes to cook the flesh, which he gave to the people to eat. He then followed Elijah and became his disciple.

To anyone who has read the Gospels, there is a sense of familiarity in this story. Elijah's throwing of his cloak is more dramatic than Jesus' call of his disciples, but the overall effect is the same. Elisha leaves his home and family and sets off to be the disciple and eventual successor to Elijah.

In outward appearance, there is a world of a difference between Elisha's experience and ours. He, like the Galilean fishermen, was called to be a wandering preacher and prophet. We, for the most part, stay at home and strive to serve God in our normal lives. He sacrificed his greatest possessions to God, we are taught to keep them well as part of our Christian stewardship. At a deeper level, though, there is (or should be) a close similarity. Elisha could sacrifice his oxen and their gear because he already saw them not as his, but as God's. He was able to leave home because his first commitment was not to his farm work but to God.

You could say that the call of Elisha only confirmed what was already true of him: that God was his first love. Even though we are unlikely to be called to drop everything and head off into the wide blue yonder, it is worth asking whether we could. Are we so wedded to our present lives and possessions that God could not separate us from them? Or do we truly see them as his, held in trust and used for his service?

A reflection

All things come from you, and of your own do we give you . . .

Alternative Service Book

1 Kings 20:22,23,28 (REB)

Limited God

[A] prophet came to the king of Israel and advised him, 'Build up your forces; you know what you must do. At the turn of the year, the king of Aram will renew the attack.' The ministers of the king of Aram gave him this advice: 'Their gods are gods of the hills; that is why they are too strong for us. Let us fight them in the plain, and then we shall have the upper hand . . .' The man of God came to the king of Israel and said, 'This is the word of the Lord: The Aramaeans may think that the Lord is a god of the hills and not a god of the valleys; but I shall give all this great host into your hands and you will know that I am the Lord.'

Up to now, the story has focused closely on Elijah, but in this chapter the perspective draws back and shows us something more of the background. Ahab has been at war with the king of Aram, and with God's help (delivered through the words of an unnamed prophet) he has won a great victory. (God still hasn't given up on him.) Now another battle looms.

The Aramaeans' idea is a good one. Everyone knew that gods ruled their own little territories. If Israel's god was strong in the mountains, then he would likely be weak in the plains. They have no understanding of the claim of the Lord to be the God of the whole earth. They are about to be brutally enlightened.

The ancient Aramaeans had an excuse—but we still make the same mistake. How many times do we imagine that God, who is all very

well in church, has no place in our other activities? We may not actually say that, because we know better, but when we look closely at our lives, don't we find that there are some areas that we don't think suitable for prayer, or some activities we would rather God had no part in?

It may be we want to keep him away from things we are ashamed of, or that we are secretly afraid he won't or can't be any help. But for whatever reason, our idea of God is often too limited.

A way to pray

Look again, and see where you try to limit God—and then make the effort to acknowledge him there as well.

1 Kings 21:1–7 (REB)

Abuse of power

Some time later there occurred an incident involving Naboth of Jezreel, who had a vineyard in Jezreel adjoining the palace of King Ahab of Samaria. Ahab made a proposal to Naboth: 'Your vineyard is close to my palace; let me have it for a garden, and I shall give you a better vineyard in exchange for it or, if you prefer, I shall give you its value in silver.' But Naboth answered, 'The Lord forbid that I should surrender to you land which has always been in my family.' Ahab went home sullen and angry because Naboth had refused to let him have his ancestral holding. He took to his bed, covered his face, and refused to eat. When his wife Jezebel came in to him and asked, 'Why this sullenness, and why do you refuse to eat?' he replied, 'I proposed that Naboth of Jezreel should let me have his vineyard at its value or, if he liked, in exchange for another; but he refused to let me have it.' 'Are you or are you not king in Israel?' retorted Jezebel. 'Come, eat and take heart; I shall make you a gift of the vineyard of Naboth of Jezreel.'

So Jezebel has Naboth executed on false charges, and Ahab happily receives the vineyard as a gift from his wife. It's a story as old as the land, and one which many people could tell of their neighbours today, in many parts of the world. It is a strange fact that power really does corrupt. Or at least, power is always prone to be misused.

And that goes for any kind of power, including ours. But we don't have power, we might say. Yet we do. Parents have power over their children (and how often are children punished to relieve their parents' stress rather than because of real naughtiness?). Managers and foremen, supervisors and secretaries all have their own little bits of power—and can abuse it. In churches, choir leaders, organists, choristers, flower arrangers can all use their positions to exert leverage rather than to serve. And as for the clergy . . .

We may not have as much power as Ahab, or as much opportunity for corruption, but the danger exists. The only way to counter it is to learn true service.

A reflection

For the Son of Man also came not to be served, but to serve.

Mark 10:45 (RSV)

Luke 15:20–24 (RSV)

Home again

While he was yet at a distance, his father saw him and had compassion, and ran and embraced him and kissed him. And the son said to him, 'Father, I have sinned against heaven and before you; I am no longer worthy to be called your son.' But the father said to his servants, 'Bring quickly the best robe, and put it on him; and put a ring on his hand, and shoes on his feet; and bring the fatted calf and kill it, and let us eat and make merry; for this my son was dead; and is alive again; he was lost, and is found.' And they began to make merry.

When we hear again a familiar story, we can sometimes be struck by something entirely new. I have always seen the tale of the prodigal son as being about forgiveness (which it is) but today a new thought struck me. It is also about belonging.

One of Augustine's most famous sentences is the prayer, 'You have made us for yourself, O God, and our hearts are restless till they find their rest in you.' Meeting God is about coming home.

We are indeed restless in much of our lives. We are beset by worries and demands on our time, our skills and our love. But when we are with God, we should relax, for we are at home, in the bosom of the family, and have nothing to prove, no one to impress.

Today as you prepare to worship, to pray, to take Communion, think about this. In the midst of worship we are in our family, and at home, accepted for what we are.

MM

---

1 Kings 21:15,16 (REB)

Responsibility

As soon as Jezebel heard of the death of Naboth, she said to Ahab, 'Get up and take possession of the vineyard which Naboth refused to sell you, for he is no longer alive; Naboth of Jezreel is dead.' On hearing that Naboth was dead, Ahab got up and went to the vineyard to take possession.'

We can hardly help but feel contempt for Ahab. Instead of serving Israel, he sulks while his wife does murder in his name. Perhaps he didn't even allow himself to ask how Naboth had so conveniently died, so as not to have to cope with his conscience. Yet once again, writ large and unmistakeable, here is something we can recognize.

Don't we often fail to ask questions because we are afraid we know the answer—and that it will make demands on us? It could be the cheap car radio we are offered in a pub, or the way our colleague at work is always around when something goes missing. Or more commonly (and more subtly) it could be the household goods and food we use, without ever asking how they are produced, or what their effect will be. The question of how much tea growers are paid, or what conditions are like for the producers of our coffee, seems far removed from the simple joy of our early morning cuppa. And as we shake our heads sadly over pictures of yet another

polluted river, before we head for the kitchen and the washing-up detergent, are we really all that different from the king who never asked how the vineyard was so conveniently for sale?

When Ahab faces up to his duties (as in the war against Aram) he finds that God is with him. When he lets himself sink into self-pity and effectively hands over his kingdom to Jezebel, disaster falls. Yet he never seems to learn the lesson that to shirk responsibility is to turn his back on God and on himself.

Yet as the theologian Emil Brunner once pointed out, to be human is to be responsible; for ourselves, for each other and for the world—responsible to God.

A reflection

In what ways are you tempted to shirk your responsibilities? Focus on them in your prayers.

1 Kings 21:17–21,27–29 (REB)

Never too late

The word of the Lord came to Elijah the Tishbite: 'Go down at once to King Ahab of Israel, who is in Samaria; you will find him in Naboth's vineyard, where he has gone to take possession ... Say to him, "This is the word of the Lord: Where dogs licked the blood of Naboth, there dogs will lick your blood." ' Ahab said to Elijah, 'So you have found me, my enemy.' 'Yes,' he said, 'because you have sold yourself to do what is wrong in the eyes of the Lord. I shall bring disaster on you; I shall sweep you away and destroy every mother's son of the house of Ahab in Israel, whether under the protection of the family or not ...' When Ahab heard Elijah's words, he tore his clothes, put on sackcloth, and fasted; he lay down in his sackcloth and went about moaning. The word of the Lord came to Elijah the Tishbite: 'Have you seen how Ahab has humbled himself before me? Because he has thus humbled himself, I shall not bring disaster on his house in his own lifetime, but in that of his son.'

We often get the impression that God in the Old Testament is seen as implacably angry. But that isn't true. The prophecies of judgment so often come about not because God won't listen to repentance, but because his hearers are implacably sinful. At last, Ahab repents, and doom is averted, at least for a time.

Don't forget that the Old Testament knows almost nothing of real life after death. For Ahab, the words of God are equivalent to salvation. He has repented and God has responded with forgiveness.

First, though, he had to have his nose rubbed in his misdeeds. It is easy to fall into a habit of ignoring God,

perhaps in only one area of our lives. Then we become accustomed to sin—what the Bible calls hardness of heart. God's only way to get through to us is to deal harshly with us and force us to turn back to him. It's painful, but it's grace.

A reflection
Have there been times in your life when God has dealt with you harshly? Do you have the courage to thank him for the lesson?

1 Kings 22:6–9 (REB)

Comfort and truth

The king of Israel assembled the prophets, some four hundred of them, and asked, 'Shall I attack Ramoth-gilead or not?' 'Attack,' was the answer; 'the Lord will deliver it into your majesty's hands.' Jehoshaphat asked, 'Is there no other prophet of the Lord here through whom we may seek guidance?' 'There is one more,' the king of Israel answered, 'through whom we may seek guidance of the Lord, but I hate the man, because he never prophesies good for me, never anything but evil. His name is Micaiah son of Imlah.' Jehoshaphat exclaimed, 'My lord king, let no such word pass your lips!' So the king of Israel called one of his eunuchs and told him to fetch Micaiah son of Imlah with all speed.

A friend of mine once heard that his friend was heading off to a hotel with a woman other than his wife. There was much nudging and winking. But my friend jumped into his car and arrived at the hotel first. He confronted the couple, pointed out the consequences for his friend's marriage, and the two separated, never to meet again. Years later, the would-be adulterer is still happily married, and is glad that he was stopped. But he still can't bring himself to speak to my friend.

What we always want to hear are words of comfort and approval. But what we often need to hear are words of truth. Ahab could summon four hundred prophets of God to bless his alliance with the king of Judah in yet another war against Aram. But what could he expect to hear from prophets who had survived the period of Baal-worship? Jehoshaphat could smell a rat and wanted the truth. Eventually it came: 'The Lord has decreed disaster for you,' said Micaiah.

But even the truth is not always enough—Ahab would not listen (it was four hundred to one!) and so went to battle. Despite his precautions, he was killed. He preferred comfort to truth.

A prayer
Lord, give me friends with enough love to speak the truth, and give me enough courage to hear it, and to act upon it.

1 Kings 22:13–17 (REB)

Speaking truth

The messenger sent to fetch Micaiah told him that the prophets had unanimously given the king a favourable answer. 'And mind you agree with them,' he added. 'As the Lord lives,' said Micaiah, 'I shall say only what the Lord tells me to say.' When he came into the king's presence, the king asked, 'Micaiah, shall I attack Ramoth-gilead, or shall I refrain?' 'Attack and win the day,' he replied, 'the Lord will deliver it into your hands.' 'How often must I adjure you,' said the king, 'to tell me nothing but the truth in the name of the Lord?' Then Micaiah said, 'I saw all Israel scattered on the mountains, like sheep without a shepherd; and I heard the Lord say, "They have no master; let them go home in peace."'

If we need sometimes to hear the truth spoken, we need also to be speakers of the truth. And there are times, as Micaiah found, when speaking the truth is a dangerous business. In fact, he was thrown in gaol for it. Yet it isn't quite as simple as it seems.

'Speaking the truth' is not simply saying, 'Awful,' when a friend asks how they look in their new dress. The real criterion is speaking the truth for another person's genuine good. Micaiah told Ahab the bad news because it was in Ahab's interest to know it. When we tell someone that their driving is dangerous, it is in their interest (and ours if we are with them!). Insulting their taste in clothes is merely destructive and unhelpful.

There are plenty of people who are willing to upset others and say, 'I was only being truthful.' But they weren't; they were being vindictive. God's people are called to be truthful, not so as to hurt, but so as to heal, uncomfortable though it may be. That means sometimes being painfully truthful to a friend, sometimes it means exposing the false standards of society. But always it is to turn people to the ways of God.

A question

What is the difference between being pedantically honest and 'speaking the truth in love'?

2 Kings 1:2–4 (REB)

Consequences

When Ahaziah fell through a latticed window in his roof-chamber in Samaria and injured himself, he sent messengers to enquire of Baal-zebub the god of Ekron whether he would recover from this injury. The angel of the Lord ordered Elijah the Tishbite to go and meet the messengers of the king of Samaria and say to them, 'Is there no God in Israel, that you go to consult Baal-zebub the god of Ekron? For what you have done the word of the Lord to your master is this: You will not rise from the bed where you are lying; you will die.' With that Elijah departed.

After Ahab's death, his son Ahaziah ruled for seventeen years, and seems to have been no great improvement. The last straw comes when he is willing to entrust his life to a false god.

Nowadays we might ask what chance he had, given the parents he had, and the example they and their court must have set him. The answer is not simple. Everyone is responsible for their own deeds; yet the way we act is influenced by the teaching and example of many others: our parents and teachers, our friends and neighbours, the whole ethos of our nation. It is probably fair to say that not only are we responsible for our own actions, but also in some degree for the actions of others.

We live in a very individualistic age. Everyone is seen as the master of their own fate. But it simply isn't true. We are all connected, and our words and deeds have consequences for the lives of others in ways we find hard to imagine. Of course, that doesn't mean we bear the guilt or take the credit for the way others behave. But it does mean that we cast an influence—for good or ill—by all that we do.

A prayer

Father, make me aware of the influence I have on others, and let me be an example of your love.

2 Kings 2:7–14 (REB)

End of an episode

Fifty of the prophets followed [Elijah and Elisha], and stood watching as the two of them stopped by the Jordan. Elijah took his cloak, rolled it up, and struck the water with it. The water divided to right and left, and both crossed over on dry ground. While they were crossing, Elijah said to Elisha, 'Tell me what I can do for you before I am taken from you.' Elisha said, 'Let me inherit a double share of your spirit.' 'You have asked a hard thing,' said Elijah. 'If you see me taken from you, your wish will be granted; if you do not, it will not be granted.' They went on, talking as they went, and suddenly there appeared a chariot of fire and horses of fire, which separated them from one another, and Elijah was carried up to heaven in a whirlwind. At the sight Elisha cried out, 'My father, my father, the chariot and the horsemen of Israel!' and he saw him no more. He clutched hold of his mantle and tore it in two. He picked up the cloak which had fallen from Elijah, and went back and stood on the bank of the Jordan. There he struck the water with Elijah's cloak, saying as he did so, 'Where is the Lord, the God of Elijah?' As he too struck the water, it divided to right and left, and he crossed over.

The double share that Elisha asks for doesn't mean that he wants to be twice the prophet Elijah was. It is simply a way of asking to inherit Elijah's business as God's prophet to Israel. And he does. As he strikes the water, and the Jordan rolls back, the watching prophets exclaim that the spirit of Elijah is still here. Indeed it is, for it is God's Spirit, and the work of God continues. The story of God has no neat ending, but goes on throughout history. With the passing of Elijah, the story does not end, but simply enters a new episode. For Christians, the story has an added meaning. Since Pentecost, the Spirit who was in Elijah is the Spirit of the church. All of us bear the prophet's mantle. If the waters don't roll back before us, that is nothing compared to the fact that the word of God is still spoken; by him to us, and by us to others.

Matthew 18:21–22 (JB)

Forgiveness

Peter went up to [Jesus] and said, 'Lord, how often must I forgive my brother if he wrongs me? As often as seven times?' Jesus answered, 'Not seven, I tell you, but seventy-seven times.'

C.S. Lewis once reflected on why the creeds say, 'I believe in the forgiveness of sins.' Surely that was so obvious that it hardly needed reciting? The whole of Christianity is about having our sins forgiven. But then he came to the conclusion that it is not forgiveness of our sins that we need to be reminded of, but our forgiving of others' sins against us.

I'm sure he was right. How many times have we heard objections to Jesus' command to forgive our enemies? 'Surely you can't forgive murderers! What about Hitler? What about the IRA?' When people raise the hard cases, it's usually because they want excuses not to do it at all.

Yet the command stands. Those who know they are forgiven must be springs of forgiveness themselves. So how do we do it?

Lewis said it was a matter of practice. Learn to forgive the little wrongs, and forgiveness becomes habitual, and the greater wrongs are easier to forgive. That is true. Yet there's more to it than that. It is also a matter of prayer.

Don't pray for the ability to forgive. Pray for the people you know you ought to forgive. When we hold up even our enemies to the love of God, it becomes very difficult not to begin to have some of that love for them ourselves. All true forgiveness begins with God, and so begins with prayer.

MM

Prayers for the Decade of Evangelism

Almighty God, give us your Holy Spirit so that we may have power
to speak about you and not be afraid to spread your Word
throughout the world. May we ourselves show the world your
Word through our actions and know that you are always with us.
Through Jesus Christ our Lord. Amen.

Church of Melanesia

Father, pour out your Spirit upon your people,
and grant to us:
a new vision of your glory;
a new faithfulness to your Word;
a new consecration to your service;
that your life may grow among us,
and your kingdom come; through Jesus Christ
our Lord. Amen.

Church in Australia

Almighty God, you have sent your Son into this world to show
your love for us, and you are still working and wishing that all
people of the world may enjoy perfect reconciliation and
communion with you. Grant that we may be enlightened to
discern your work here on earth and make us able to give
ourselves in the Decade of Evangelism, to become witnesses to
your work, and to share with all people the fulfilment of your
eternal Kingdom, through the only High Priest, your Son, Jesus
Christ our Lord. Amen.

Church of Japan

We acknowledge these prayers with thanks to the Decade of Evangelism, The
Anglican Communion, Partnership House, 157 Waterloo Road, London SE1 8UT.

Praying the Scriptures

For the Christian the Word of the Lord is eternal. The revelation of the Lord came at a particular time and place and always related to the circumstances of his people, in the Old Testament, in Jesus Christ himself, or in the Word which expressed and defined the early Christian community. The Word of the Lord licked the community into shape—reluctantly, for they were as slow to listen as we are. Gradually they learned the nature of God, of human community, of the fullness of God's love in Christ, and how human beings can respond to that love in their relationship to God and to each other.

And yet it was not only to them that it came. It was addressed also to us, for their temptations, foibles, squabbles, infidelities, problems are ours too. Their history is our history too. Building a Christian community is slow work. If we are to come closer to God, to add our straw or flake to the Christian community, we can do so only by listening to his Word, by reflecting on it and praying about it.

These excerpts from Scripture are all concerned with the Word of God, its power and its nature. First comes a passage from Scripture. Then comes a little comment, which attempts to situate the passage in its time and place, and to see what message it holds. Finally comes a verse or two from Scripture (often from the Psalms, the prayerbook of Israel) which may form a little nugget for thought or reflection about the themes found in the main passage.

Prayer about these passages needs thoughtful reading. Do not hurry. Just stop, reflect, re-read, refer back to the passage of Scripture addressed to you by the Lord, and talk to him about it. If the comment is helpful, reflect on it. If the comment is unhelpful, converse with the Lord about why it misses the point. The final nugget may be a little line to learn by heart and carry about during the day as a reminder and a refresher of the time spent with God.

Henry Wansbrough

Genesis 1:24,25 (NJB)

God's creative Word

God said, 'Let the earth produce every kind of living creature in its own species: cattle, creeping things and wild animals of all kinds.' And it was so ... God saw that it was good.

The Bible gives us a simplified picture of how the universe came to be, God supreme and smoothly issuing commands which are equally smoothly accomplished.

Is this a magical world, out of touch with reality? We know about the Big Bang, how countless millions of years ago something happened from which the universe as we know it came to be, and still continues to expand to unimaginable distances of light-years. Are the stories of creation untrue, then? No, they are simply another way of looking at the same facts.

The trees as we see them, the grass, the cornflakes in our packets, the spider's web in the corner—all came to be, and exist from moment to moment, because God wishes them to be so. If I cease to think a thought, that the girl's hair looks like strands of gold as she skips in the sunset, then that thought ceases to exist (even though the hair, the girl and the sunset all remain). Just so, if God should cease to create the trees, the grass, the cornflakes, the spider's web, and hold them in existence, then there would simply be nothing there.

The Big Bang was the beginning, but not *the* beginning. Perhaps, instead of the Big Bang and the creative Word of God, we should think of God's Great Roar, whose sound still continues, ebbing and flowing with the rhythms of the universe. But it was no meaningless roar, rather a thoughtful, loving and planned expression of thought, a Word. God created deliberately, with all the care of forming a Word. 'God spoke and it was so, and God saw that it was good.'

A reflection

By the Word of the Yahweh the heavens were made, by the breath of his mouth all their array.

Psalm 33:6

Jeremiah 18:1 (NJB)

The prophetic Word

The word that came to Jeremiah from Yahweh as follows, 'Get up and make your way down to the potter's house, and there I shall tell you what I have to say.'

More than most of the prophets, Jeremiah seems to pluck the Word of the Lord out of the circumstances of his life.

He goes to watch the potter and sees God's message about Israel in the way the potter shapes different pots for different purposes.

He goes to the market and sees God's message in two baskets of figs, one ripe, the other putrid: just so, some of the members of God's holy people are good, some bad.

If we keep our ears and eyes open, the Word of the Lord may come to us in all kinds of guises: God's own fatherly criticism in the angry word of a colleague; the unfailing love of God in the affectionate word of a friend; God's warning in the shape of a narrow escape; divine forgiveness in the acceptance of an apology. As we reflect on them we can see that all these are signs of God's love and care.

The Word of God is not just a spoken or written word, but can be heard in all the chances and encounters of daily life. We can pray about all the events of the day, reflect on them in the quiet of the evening. Blind and stubborn as we so often are, especially in the heat of action, we can share these events, these joys and setbacks, with the Lord, and see what Word of his they contain, what the Lord is trying to say to us.

A reflection

In the way of your instruction lies my joy, a joy beyond all wealth. I will ponder your precepts and fix my gaze on your paths.

Psalm 119:14–15

Isaiah 55:10–11 (NJB)

God's Word of promise

As the rain and the snow come down from the sky and do not return before having watered the earth, fertilising it and making it germinate to provide seed for the sower and food to eat, so it is with the word that goes from my mouth.

In the Old Testament God's Word of promise is the backbone of his people's life, providing the structure and framework of all their thought and activity.

The promise to Abraham that his descendants should be as numerous as the sand on the seashore, the permanence of the protection which this implies, sustained Israel through all the vicissitudes of history. They were sure that God would deliver them—provided that they were faithful in their response to him.

Then the promise that David's line would not fail gave them confidence throughout the period of the monarchy. In the anguish of the Babylonian exile it was the promise of vindication, the messianic promise, which sustained them: the belief that in spite of their failure God would not desert them but would—in his own good time—transform the world and rid it of sorrow, suffering and death.

This hope was constantly reiterated by a succession of prophetic words. God's promise beat upon their ears age after age. So too for us,

God's Word of promise sustains us. The meaningless death of an innocent loved one, betrayal by friends, personal failure and incompetence—whatever disaster befall, we still have God's promise to fall back on.

For those with Christian faith no disaster can be ultimate or permanent. God sustains the world. He can draw good out of evil. He promises never to desert those who put their trust in him. And his Word has power: it can never be invalidated. Just as with the Word of Creation, the mere speaking of it guarantees its accomplishment.

A reflection

Keep in mind your promise to your servant on which I have built my hope. It is my comfort in distress that your promise gives me life.

Psalm 119:49,50

Exodus 34:6,7 (NJB)

God's Word for himself: the Name of God

Then Yahweh passed before [Moses] and called out, 'Yahweh, Yahweh, God of tenderness and compassion, slow to anger, rich in faithful love and constancy, maintaining his faithful love to thousands, forgiving fault, crime and sin, yet letting nothing go unchecked.'

If you don't know somebody's name, you have little control over a person, as any teacher can tell from experience. So if you don't want to give yourself at all, just refuse to give your name.

At the beginning Abraham did not know the name of his Protector God, and often in the first stories of the Bible God refuses to give his name. It was only at the burning bush that the personal Name of 'Yahweh' was revealed, and even then it remained incomprehensible and perhaps meaningless. God would interpret it only as 'I am who I am'; this gives little away!

But later on, in the desert, when Israel has committed itself to God (and also fallen totally by its unfaithfulness over the golden calf) God does reveal the meaning of his Name. This is the gift by God of himself to his people, granting them a power even over him, a pledge of intimacy and favour.

The revelation of the meaning of the Name is itself an act of love. It is as a God of mercy and tenderness, love and compassion that God makes himself known. This passage echoes down the Bible. It is quoted again and again within the Bible. That was how God came to be known as his love was revealed in all the aspects of its richness.

The actual name 'Yahweh' remains a mystery. To the Jews of recent times it is too sacred to be pronounced. Awe of God has taken precedence over loving intimacy. But the Name is still written, as a testimony of the abiding bond of love with Israel.

A prayer

I shall sing the faithful love of Yahweh for ever, from age to age my lips shall declare your constancy, for you have said, 'Love is built to last for ever.'

Psalm 89:1,2

St Mary Magdalen 99

Psalm 119:92,93 (NJB)

God's Word as Law

Had your Law not been my delight, I would have perished in my misery. I shall never forget your precepts, for by them you have given me life.

For most of us law is a restricting factor, defining the limits beyond which we may not go, restraining excesses and even cramping our style. For Israel in the Old Testament the Word of the Lord (which was his Law—and the Ten Commandments are called the 'Ten Words') was a delight.

Firstly, the Law was a revelation of God himself, communicating to Israel his own standards and requirements. The demands you make on people show the sort of person you are, and the demands God makes on his people show what he himself is. Especially is this the case because the Law lays down the terms of the treaty or marriage contract between God and Israel. It details what sort of conduct in Israel is necessary for Israel to be God's people, to live together with God, to have God in their midst.

He cannot be in the midst of a people wholly foreign to him, and with a people wholly foreign to his ways there could be no bond. 'Be holy as I am holy' is not an arbitrary demand, but is a condition of associating with God. You must like the way your spouse behaves, and to encourage your spouse to behave in the way you find charming and lovely is itself an expression of love.

Secondly, the Law gives the people of Israel a chance to respond to God in this love, to show their own affection for God. So obedience to the Law is not a grim obligation, but a joyful response to God's initiative.

A reflection

Your commandments fill me with delight, I love them dearly.

Psalm 119:47

John 1:1,14 (NJB)

Christ, the Word of the Father

In the beginning was the Word; the Word was with God and the Word was God.... The Word became flesh, he lived among us and we saw his glory.

The fourth Gospel opens with a prologue to set the scene of the whole Gospel. The theme of the Gospel is the revelation of the awesome divine glory of God made visible in Christ Jesus, and these few verses give the key in the magnificent imagery of a poem.

The first phrase links back to the story of creation, 'in the beginning', placing the Word alone on the stage. Is this the first moment of creation, with God's creative Word poised to form the universe? Or is it the moment before creation, when the mysterious inner life of God existed alone in eternal timelessness?

John's writing is so rich and allusive that it is always rash to rule out entirely the possibility that both senses are meant. The translation of the second phrase is an impoverishment of the thought of the evangelist's Greek. He wrote 'the Word was towards God', suggesting a partnership, the Word turned towards God, receiving all from God, steadily and uninterruptedly in communication with God.

The third phrase does not say that God and the Word are identical, the same being, but 'what God was, the Word was'. The Word has all the divine quality, power and substance. John chooses the expression 'Word' to convey the idea of identity in difference. My word expresses my thought, or indeed myself. It draws all its life from me, and needs to be continuously spoken by me. It is under my control and yet is not the same as myself; it has a certain being of its own, which yet is mine.

Just so with this Word of God, which has come among us and so made visible his glory.

A reflection

The grass withers, the flower fades, but the word of our God remains for ever.

Isaiah 40:8

Ezekiel 36:24-28 (NJB)

A new heart

For I shall take you from among the nations and gather you back from all the countries, and bring you home to your own country. I shall pour clean water over you and you will be cleansed; I shall give you a new heart, and put a new spirit in you; I shall remove the heart of stone from your bodies and give you a heart of flesh instead. I shall put my spirit in you, and make you keep my laws, and respect and practise my judgements. You will live in the country which I gave your ancestors.

Ezekiel proclaimed this hope to his fellow-exiles, dreary and depressed beside the waters of Babylon. They had been exiled from their country across a trackless desert. Everything they relied on had crumbled to dust—the holy city, the temple, the monarchy. What had become of the promises of God which were centred on these institutions? How, in an alien land, could they worship the God they had betrayed?

A way to worship and to pray:

Lord God, your people of the Old Covenant deserted you and were unfaithful, running after other gods and the distractions and temptations of the world. As we look back now at their story in Scripture we can see how you admonished them and attempted to lure them back to yourself. Yet even the material remains in your Holy Land show their idolatry and the way they relied on superstition and charms, even when paying lip-service to you. We too chase after the gods of this world: power, position, money, physical gratification. And all the while you are there, waiting for us, reminding us, though we come so rarely to speak to you and bathe in your light.

You promised not to destroy them, and to correct them only as a father corrects his child. When you had no alternative but to destroy the symbols of nationhood, you yourself took the first step to renew your bond with them in an even richer way. You promised to cleanse them and pour clean water over them, giving them a new heart by which they could know and love you individually. Wait for me, too, and renew my heart. Rid me of the shallowness of my observance, and make my love for you vibrant and all-embracing.

HW

John 1:14 (trans. HW)

He tented among us

The Word became flesh, he tented among us and we saw his glory, the glory that he has from the Father as the only Son of the Father.

The climax of the Prologue of John expresses the climax of history. 'Word' is the expression chosen by John to express the very real yet immaterial existence of that which exists within the divinity but is not identical with the Father, that which is in a vibrant relationship with God and is all that God is. And now—the opposite extreme—this is said to become 'flesh', a word regarded as far too coarse ever to be used in the polite conversation of previous generations!

The Word took on the full reality of human nature, with physical pain and pleasure, sexual desire and control, hunger and repletion, misery and delight, surprise and disappointment, the final agony and humiliation of death. Two hints remind us that this climax of history is also the fulfilment of Judaism.

First, the word translated 'tented' is used of dwelling in a tent, and recalls the tent of meeting in the desert during the Exodus, which remained the centre of God's presence among his people, the meeting-place of Israel with God. At the same time the word used in Greek has the same basic letters, so the same basic sound, as the Hebrew word for God's glory, *shekinah*; this must have been deliberate.

Secondly, 'we saw his glory' is an awesome phrase. The glory of God is so frightening that any human being flees in terrified reverence. No human being can see God and live; to see his glory is almost as fearsome, driving anyone to hide in the dust or the crevices of the rock 'in terror of Yahweh, at the brilliance of his majesty' (Isaiah 2:19). This glory, though untamed, has now been made humanly visible in Jesus Christ.

A prayer

God, you are my God, I pine for you, my heart thirsts for you, my body longs for you, as a land parched, dreary and waterless. Thus I have gazed on you in the sanctuary, seeing your power and your glory.

Psalm 63:1,2

2 Corinthians 1:18–20 (NJB)

Christ, the 'Yes' of the Father

As surely as God is trustworthy, what we say to you is not both Yes and No. The Son of God, Jesus Christ, who was proclaimed to you by us . . . was never Yes-and-No; his nature is all Yes. For in him is found the Yes to all God's promises and therefore it is 'through him' that we answer 'Amen' to give praise to God.

Paul is replying to the charge of instability. It seems that the Corinthians had charged him with needlessly and capriciously changing his plans. He replies that he shares in the firmness of Christ, who is the firmness, the confirmation of God's promises. It is Christ who makes God's promises firm by bringing them to their fulfilment.

The clue to the full understanding of the richness of Paul's thought is that the Hebrew word 'Amen' means strength, firmness, truth, stability—everything, in fact, that builds confidence and reliance. It is also, of course, the word used in public prayer, by which the listeners (by answering 'Amen') take on the prayer for themselves and confirm it as their own. So it is Jesus who provides us with the certainty of all God's promises. Just as in the public prayer of the Church there is a great chorus of 'Amen' to conclude a prayer and take it on board for everyone, so Jesus is the last word, who brings satisfaction and finality to God's Word of promise.

Paul may even be alluding to the fact that the great prayer of Christianity, the Eucharist, already in his time concluded 'through him', and received the response of the great 'Amen'. So, by this final 'Amen', we echo the fulfilment of God's promises in Jesus.

A prayer

. . . through him, with him, in him, in the unity of the Holy Spirit, all honour and glory is yours, almighty Father, for ever and ever. 'Amen'.

Eucharistic Prayer: Roman Missal

Hebrews 4:12,13 (NJB)

The two-edged sword

The Word of God is something alive and active. It cuts more incisively than any two-edged sword: it can seek out the place where soul is divided from spirit, or joints from marrow, it can pass judgement on secret emotions and thoughts. No created thing is hidden from him; everything is uncovered and stretched fully open to the eyes of the one to whom we must give account of ourselves.

The author of the Letter to the Hebrews is referring to the passages of Scripture which provide the standards for his readers. They were faint-hearted and dissatisfied, looking over their shoulders at a situation they had left behind. Sternly, the writer reminds them that God has given us aims and guidance for our way of life, and that with him there is no deception.

How can we know God's will in the confusing hubbub of the market-place? Scripture does not provide easy, automatic answers. To jab at the Scriptures for an answer with the point of a pin is mere superstition, and to tear a solitary text out of its context is not much better.

We need to understand, to love and to reflect on the Scriptures, re-cognizing that they reveal the mind and the power of their divine author. This is why they can be our judge. A human judge can be hoodwinked and deceived. A human partner in con-versation can be flattered or diverted from the truth. But with a text that is the Word of God there is no decep-tion. It speaks—and I have only myself to deceive.

But there is no point, because God cannot be deceived. And the Word of God is his instrument, his extended arm to me. The tenderness and for-giveness of God are all very well (and glorious). But only the blindest and most complacent Christian would even want to be free of judgment as well.

In the Gospels we see Jesus jud-ging, or, rather, people judging them-selves by their reaction to him, as they accept or reject him. As he is the Word of God, so we meet God's Word as we turn to the Gospels. As we read, in silence and in prayer, we hear the judgment of God.

A prayer

I have moulded myself to your judgements. I cling to your instructions, Yahweh, do not disappoint me. I run the way of your commandments.

Psalm 119:30,31

Isaiah 58:6–8 (NJB)

Word of freedom

Is not this the sort of fast that pleases me: to break unjust fetters, to undo the thongs of the yoke, to let the oppressed go free, and to break all yokes? Is it not sharing your food with the hungry, and sheltering the homeless poor; if you see someone lacking clothes, to clothe him, and not to turn away from your own kin? Then your light will blaze out like the dawn and your wound be quickly healed over.

Unpopularity, persecution, mockery, failure held no fears for them. The prophets of the Old Testament proclaimed to their contemporaries how God saw the situation in their world. The Word of the Lord was that injustice was being done, that his people were enslaved.

Every now and then a figure appears in our world who speaks in the same way. William Wilberforce spoke out tirelessly, and eventually successfully, against the evils of slavery, which were simply accepted in the conventional world. A whole new frame of thinking was needed. In this century Martin Luther King was his successor, speaking out fearlessly for the rights of the oppressed black minority in the United States, and winning a whole new sensitivity by his death for his outspokenness.

In our generation perhaps it is Mother Teresa who speaks most clearly for the needs of the oppressed—in a way the conscience of the world. She speaks quietly too, and with tolerance but insistence. It is not necessarily the most strident voice which is most clearly heard.

A reflection

*For as the rain and the snow come down from the sky
and do not return before having watered the earth...
so it is with the word that goes from my mouth:
it will not return to me unfulfilled.*

Isaiah 55:10–11

1 Peter 1:23–25 (NJB)

The imperishable seed

Your new birth was not from any perishable seed but from imperishable seed, the living and enduring Word of God. For all humanity is grass, and all its beauty like the wild flower's. As grass withers, the flower fades, but the Word of the Lord remains for ever. And this Word is the Good News that has been brought to you.

This passage from the First Letter of Peter is almost a meditation on what John's Gospel has to say about the Word. Jesus is the Word made flesh, come so that all people may have life. John's Gospel hovers or circles, with the flight of the eagle, round the precious concepts of the Word, truth and eternal life. 'Consecrate them in the truth,' prays Jesus at his Last Supper, 'your word is truth'. 'You have the words of eternal life,' cries Peter to Jesus, when many of the disciples cannot accept his teaching. 'I have come so that they may have life,' says the Good Shepherd, in contrast to the thief and the hireling.

What does it mean that this Word is the imperishable seed of eternal life? The world of Jesus was a world torn by strife, beset with disasters, a web of instability and insecurity. From this Jesus claims to set his followers free. The seed of life which he sows by the Word of his Good News cannot be lost or die. This is the essence of that faith which is commitment to him. Faith is no matter of believing this proposition or believ-ing that dogma. It is a matter of trust, of whole-hearted commitment to him and to the promises of God which he mediates.

The instability of the world in which we live is no less than that of two thousand years ago. We may understand a little more about the causes of disease, disaster and death, but they still remain unavoidable, on a large scale or small. The only salva-tion remains to commit ourselves through thick and thin to the Word of the Lord.

A prayer

True to your word, support me and I shall live; do not disappoint me of my hope.

Psalm 119:116

Revelation 19:11–13 (NJB)

The rider of the Apocalypse

And now I saw heaven open, and a white horse appear; its rider was called Trustworthy and True; in uprightness he judges and makes war. His eyes were flames of fire, and he was crowned with many coronets; the name written on him was known only to himself, his cloak was soaked in blood. He is known by the name, The Word of God.

The Book of Revelation offers a series of powerful, often frightening, images of conflict and bloodshed. These images predict the life of the Church down the ages. Christians are always in conflict with the powers of darkness and suffering from them, but secure in the knowledge that in the end neither those powers nor anything in the whole of creation will ever be able to separate them from 'the love of God, known to us in Christ Jesus our Lord' (Romans 8:39).

Several times in the course of descriptions of the conflict, the persecution suffered by God's faithful is said to be 'for the sake of the Word of God'. Just so, in Mark's Gospel, the Christian is exhorted to be true 'for my sake and for the sake of the Gospel'. Now, as the final scenes begin, we see the Word of God triumphant. This must be Jesus himself, personifying God's Truth and the Truth of the Gospel.

The powers of darkness nowadays may be there in external temptations to compromise, by dubious business partnership or by sexual infidelity. Or I shall encounter them within myself as I struggle to be true to my standards, to fulfil my resolutions, to be faithful to prayer, and to combat my faults.

This vision of the triumph of the Word of God, Trustworthy and True, must be an inspiration in our battle to be true to the Word which we have received. The fact that 'his cloak was soaked in blood' suggests that the rider did not himself escape unscathed. Primarily the blood is the blood of his enemies. But we cannot expect an easy triumph—nor to escape without wounds of failure and suffering.

A reflection

Your Word is a lamp for my feet, a light on my path.

Psalm 119:105

John 17:11–19 (cut) (NJB)

True to his Name

I am no longer in the world, but they are in the world, and I am coming to you. Holy Father, keep those you have given me true to your name, so that they may be one like us. While I was with them, I kept those you had given me true to your name . . . Now I am coming to you and I say these things in the world to share my joy with them to the full . . . Consecrate them in the truth; your word is truth. As you sent me into the world, I have sent them into the world, and for their sake I consecrate myself so that they too may be consecrated in truth.

Praying the Word:

Holy Father, in your Son Jesus Christ you revealed to us the fullness of your love. In this prayer of his at his Last Supper with his disciples he prayed that we should consecrate ourselves in truth, make ourselves holy and dedicated to his and to your truth.

Especially at the Eucharist you give us the opportunity to consecrate ourselves with him in his final and total offering of himself. He dedicated himself to your truth, uncompromising in the face of mockery, disgrace, physical pain and even seeming failure of his work for you. In all this he was suffused by your love and drawn on by obedience to your will. Knowing the humiliation and suffering which awaited him, he still prayed to share your joy with us.

In your love for us, grant me the courage to yield myself to truth, to dedicate myself in the Eucharist with your Son. No more compromise or evasion of the truth about myself! Give me the courage to accept whatever you may send. I cannot tell what you have in store for me, but like your Son Jesus, know only that you love me with a Father's care, and that whatever you send me will be for the best for me. Let this be my joy!

HW

School of Prayer— Part 2

Prayer, according to the fifteenth-century writer Thomas à Kempis, is an art form. It needs to be learned. That is why, during Lent this year, BRF readers enrolled for a School of Prayer in that, for fourteen days, we looked together at Jesus' response to his disciples' request: Lord, teach us to pray.

Basing our studies and meditations on phrases from the Lord's Prayer, we noted that prayer begins by relating to God as a trustworthy parent-figure, it includes worship, asking, listening, dependency on God, repenting, forgiving and being forgiven. At the end of the fourteen days, we realized that we had only scratched the surface; that there was so much more to learn. That was when the School of Prayer part 2 was conceived.

This 'term' there are two subjects on our syllabus: Preparing to pray and the Holy Spirit's role in our prayer life. Under the general heading *Preparing to pray*, we shall spend one week taking a further look at Jesus' teaching and discovering for ourselves that his seemingly simple suggestions make a great deal of difference to the effectiveness of our times of quiet with God: finding a place and a time to pray; developing a sense of alertness, having high expectations, learning to take fasting seriously.

During the second week, we shall focus on the Holy Spirit and discover that without him we cannot pray. The Holy Spirit is the One who gives us access to the

Father, who, seeing our helplessness, not only teaches us to pray but prays in us and for us and through us. He is the One who knows the mind of Christ, who can reveal Jesus' thoughts and desires to us, who prompts us to pray for particular people and situations at precisely the right time. As Thomas Merton once put it: 'It is the Spirit of God that must teach us who Christ is and form Christ in us.'[1]

Like last time, the School of Prayer notes will fall into four parts: a few verses from the Bible, a comment from me, a piece of homework and a prayer or suggestion for meditation. Readers who commit themselves to all four sections will benefit most.

Although the content will seem very basic to some people, I make no apologies for going back to basics. I have found that while I have been writing the notes, revising familiar truths has been a salutary experience. From somewhere deep inside me has come an echo of the disciples' prayer: 'Lord, teach me to pray.' That heart-cry has given birth to others: Help me to find a new rhythm which works for this phase of my life. Help me to create a quiet place where I can encounter you.

These personal *cris-de-coeur* fill me with a sense of excitement

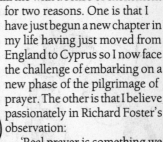

for two reasons. One is that I have just begun a new chapter in my life having just moved from England to Cyprus so I now face the challenge of embarking on a new phase of the pilgrimage of prayer. The other is that I believe passionately in Richard Foster's observation:

'Real prayer is something we learn.'[2]

Richard Foster explains why this realization proved to be so liberating for him:

'I was set free to question, to experiment, even to fail, for I knew I was learning.'[3]

It is my hope that readers, similarly, will question and

experiment. One of the things I have learned about prayer is the value of doing what Jesus did: spending prolonged periods alone with God.

In addition to ear-marking time for prayer each day, I look for 'Kingdom Moments' or little pools of silence which come like a gift from heaven on even the busiest days—moments when I can pause from typing at my computer, which come while I am preparing vegetables, which even came as I stood among the mountain of packing cases while we moved house.

Because the love of God is so sustaining, nourishing and magnetic, I try to carve out time for a monthly Quiet Day when I can luxuriate in the love of God, open myself afresh to his Spirit, when my spiritual and emotional batteries can be re-charged and I can seek God's wisdom and guidance.

Increasingly, Quiet Days and Quiet Mornings or Quiet Evenings are being organised by certain churches and Retreat Houses. They include coffee, a devotional talk on the subject of prayer, time for reflection, meditation and quiet prayer and quiet worship.

I recommend that readers who find their appetite for God whetted by the School of Prayer notes might join in such activities or explore the resources in their area. Attending these might then give rise to the desire to spend even longer with God—on a forty-eight hour or week-long retreat.

But all teachers of prayer emphasise the importance of the maxim: pray as you can, not as you can't. So my prayer for all those embarking on this second term in the School of Prayer is that your desire to encounter God through prayer might be re-kindled, that you may be as challenged as I have been by the basics and that you might be motivated to examine your own prayer practice and, where necessary, to change so that the place where you pray and the time when you pray may be tailor-made for this moment in time rather than for times past.

I pray, too, that, sensing afresh the relevance of the Holy Spirit's role in prayer, you may be able to pray with Dean Milner-White:

O most Holy Spirit,
possess me by your peace,
illuminate me by the truth,
fire me by your flame,
enable me by your power,
be made visible in me by your fruits,
lift me by your grace upon grace,
from glory to glory.[4]

Joyce Huggett

Footnotes

[1] Thomas Merton, *Seeds of Contemplation*

[2] Richard Foster, *Celebration of Discipline*

[3] Richard Foster, *Celebration of Discipline*

[4] Dean Eric Milner-White, *My God, My Glory*

Luke 11:1; Matthew 6:6 (GNB)

Preparing to Pray

'Lord, teach us to pray'

In response to that prayer of his disciples, Jesus stressed the importance of finding a prayer place:

'When you pray, go to your room, close the door, and pray . . . '

I find it fascinating to discover the way today's followers of Jesus have used their creativity to rise to this challenge.

An elderly lady once showed me the chair in the corner of her bedroom which was her prayer place. Although her husband was not a believer, he knew that when his wife was sitting in that chair, she was praying and was not to be disturbed. 'I go early to the office and pray before my colleagues arrive,' explained a Singaporean friend of mine who could find no place to pray in her crowded home. And, most movingly of all came the testimony of a young wife whose unemployed husband could not tolerate the thought of his wife praying. 'So I pray in front of the television when the commercials are on—that doesn't upset my husband because he thinks I'm sleeping!'

If you already have a prayer place, or if you have ever visited a building which is reserved for still prayer, you will understand why Jesus insisted that, for those who are serious about learning to pray, they should prepare a prayer place. Places which are earmarked for prayer seem to be saturated with a sense of the presence of God. This powerful, prayerful atmosphere accumulates over the years, and the more you visit such a place the more you are drawn into the grand silence of God which seems to permeate every nook and cranny of the building. Such places give rise to a heightened sense of expectancy, helping you to believe that you will encounter the God who seems to have taken up residence here in a very special way. In such places, you become acutely aware that God is waiting in the wings to listen, bless, restore, nourish and refresh you.

Homework

Find a place where you can go to be alone with God. Go to that place often and ask God to help you to develop your relationship with him there.

A prayer

Lord God, create in me such a homesickness for you that I am compelled to find a place where I can contemplate you and meet with you.

Matthew 14: 22,23 (GNB) ; Luke 6:12 (NIV)

Praying everywhere

Yesterday we reflected on Jesus' suggestion that when we pray we should go into our room and close the door. Yet Jesus was homeless—with nowhere to lay his head let alone a private room for prayer. Even so, he had many prayer places. The Garden of Gethsemane was one. That is why Judas knew where to take the soldiers on the night they captured his Master.

The hills and meadows were also places to which Jesus used to retreat. After he had fed the five thousand we read that he dismissed the crowd and then:

He went up a hill by himself to pray. When evening came, Jesus was there alone.

On another occasion:

Jesus went out to a mountainside to pray, and spent the night praying to God.

It would appear that Jesus could commune with his Father anywhere and everywhere. His prayer place was portable because he encountered his Father in his heart—the Bible's word for the innermost recesses of our being. This is the place where all real relationships are deepened. As we walk or work, we find ourselves thinking about or even talking to absent loved ones—planning what we will say to them when we next meet or write or speak on the telephone. In the same way, we can cultivate an inner sanctuary which enables us to enjoy intimacy with God anywhere, any time.

Angela Ashwin, in her helpful book on prayer, *Patterns not Padlocks*, suggests to young mums that they learn to sit down in the middle of chaos, if necessary, and make that a place of prayer. Sound advice. That is not to say that yesterday's notes are unimportant. Most of us need to meet with God in a still place before we learn to communicate with him on the way to work, at work, at the kitchen sink, in the supermarket queue. Wherever we find ourselves.

Homework
Today, whatever you are doing, try to be aware that God is with you: think about him and talk to him at odd moments of the day.

A prayer
Even when I am denied a space to be quiet with you, there is still a space inside me, Lord, an inner room where you are waiting for me, and which I can enter at any moment.

Angela Ashwin, *Patterns not Padlocks*

Matthew 6:26–30; 7:9–11 (NIV)

An expectation

Jesus not only assumes that we shall find a place to pray, he also seems to assume that our prayers will be laced with the expectation that God will act on our behalf. He emphasises that the Heavenly Father works for us unceasingly (see John 5:17). He is also committed to feed and clothe us:

Look at the birds of the air; they do not sow or reap or store away in barns, and yet your heavenly Father feeds them. Are you not much more valuable than they? . . . And why do you worry about clothes? See how the lilies of the field grow. They do not labour or spin. Yet I tell you that not even Solomon in all his splendour was dressed like one of these. If that is how God clothes the grass of the field . . . will he not much more clothe you?

Jesus insists that the heavenly Father can only give good gifts to his children:

Which of you, if his son asks for bread, will give him a stone? Or if he asks for a fish, will give him a snake? If you, then, though you are evil, know how to give good gifts to your children, how much more will your Father in heaven give good gifts to those who ask him

I am writing these notes in Cyprus where I now live. Summer has come and with it a glimpse of the first snakes. No Cypriot father worthy of the name would place into his child's outstretched hand a coiled, sleeping snake if that child asked for a fish. If any father did stoop to such foolishness and cruelty, there would be a public outcry. Yet some Christians seem to act as though they believe God to be less loving than human fathers. If they want something very much, they assume this could not possibly be God's will. Worse, they fall into the trap of believing that the opposite must be what God wants for them. They act as though they believe that God really wants them to be miserable.

Homework
Ask yourself: Do I believe God wants me, his child, to be happy?

Meditation
Do not look forward to what might happen tomorrow: the same everlasting Father who cares for you today will take care of you tomorrow and every day.
Francis de Sales

Alertness

'Look at that bush!' I said to my husband as we walked to the beach one day. The bush was a mass of flame-red flowers. Framed by the cloudless blue sky, the hibiscus had filled me with awe and wonder. It reminded me, too, of the verse we looked at yesterday when Jesus exclaimed: 'Consider the lilies ... even Solomon in all his glory was not arrayed like one of these' (Matthew 6:28–29).

Later, I watched a small boy paddle in the sea, fill his bucket with water and shingle and, with a smile of pure delight stretching from one ear to the other, bring these treasures back to his elderly grandmother. As he fingered the water and contemplated the multi-coloured stones he had captured, her wrinkled face lit up too. These two were relishing 'the now', attentive to what they could see and feel.

Jesus' invitation to 'look at the lilies' ... 'look at the birds' encourages us to do the same. Looking not only prepares us for stillness, it is, in itself, a way of praying. Some people call this mindfulness. As Brother Ramon puts it in *Heaven on Earth*, mindfulness means 'to enter into, to enjoy, to absorb what is immediately before you ...' He adds that to chop an onion, peel a turnip, grate a carrot and scrub a potato, if done in mindfulness, 'can be an act of meditation and a source of tranquillity and thankfulness'.

The secret of this kind of prayer is to be as alert to our surroundings as that little boy on the beach, to drink in the beauty before us, to pay attention to the sounds we so often ignore, to make it possible for all our senses to become aids to prayer: touch, smell, imagination, emotions.

Homework

Be still. Become attentive to the sounds around you. Ask God to make you equally attentive to his still, small voice. And today, pay attention to the smell, shape and texture of the things that you handle and take time to gaze at the world around you, thanking God for the wonder of his creation.

A prayer

For the beauty of the earth, for the beauty of the skies, For the love which from our birth over and around us lies, Lord of all, to thee we raise, this our sacrifice of praise.

Folliott Sandford Pierpoint

Matthew 26:38,39 (GNB)

Being real

Come as you are, that's how I love you,
Come as you are, feel quite at home,
Nothing can change the love that I bear you.
All will be well, just come as you are.

Paul Gurr   (© Spectrum Publications)

That is the verse of a song I love. It reminds me that Jesus wants us to know that there is only one way we can possibly come to God—and that is, just as we are. Children come to accepting parents like this. Like the family who came to tea with me recently. The father had been away on a conference for a few days while the three children and their mother had been staying first with the paternal grandparents and then with friends.

When they all met up in my home, the baby gurgled with obvious delight as he nestled in his father's arms—while from the older children tumbled story after story as they told their father about the fun they had had with his parents, the video they had seen at their friends' home, and the walk they had had that morning in the street where the little girl had been born. Eventually excitement turned to complaint: they were bored, they were hungry, they were hot: When were we going to have tea? Could they go out to the garden to play?

And as children come to loving parents just as they are, so when Jesus prayed he came to the Father stripped of all pretence, hiding nothing. We see this most starkly in the Garden of Gethsemane where 'grief and anguish' swept over him and he confessed:

'The sorrow in my heart is so great that it almost crushes me . . .' He threw himself face downwards on the ground and prayed: 'My Father, if it is possible, take this cup of suffering from me!'

Here we see Jesus being real. He becomes transparent, letting the full extent of his anguish and emotional suffering be known. And the assumption is that we will come to the Father like that—just as we are.

Homework

Jot down a few words or sentences which pin-point the way you are feeling at the moment. Give those feelings to God and thank him that he accepts you just as you are.

A prayer
*Just as I am . . .
I come.*

Mark 1:32,33,35 (NIV)

A priority

'I don't have time to pray.' That's a complaint many Christians make. Yet most of us make time for the things we really want to do. Jesus seems to assume that we will want to pray. The assumption: 'When you pray...' is a recurring theme through his teaching.

Jesus also set us an example. Although he was constantly under pressure from crowds of people, prayer came high on his list of priorities. So, at the peak of busyness, he disappeared— sometimes for a few snatched moments of prayer, sometimes for a whole Quiet Day and sometimes for a prayer vigil under the stars. Mark describes a typical day in the life of Jesus. It began in the Synagogue where he taught the congregation and dealt with a demon-possessed man (both draining occupations). He then went to the home of Simon and Andrew where he healed Simon's sick mother- in-law. After sunset:

The whole town gathered at the door, and Jesus healed many who had various diseases. He also drove out many demons . . .

Many Christians, after a day like that, would have enjoyed a lie in. But not Jesus. Very early next morning— while it was still dark, Jesus got up, left the house and went off to a solitary place, where he prayed.

Like Jesus, many of us live lives where our space is frequently invaded by needy people, by our noise-polluted society and by those we love. Like him, we need to establish a rhythm of prayer—snatching a few quiet moments alone with God, to plot into our diaries a monthly or bi-monthly Quiet Day or quiet morning or evening and maybe to tmake an annual retreat where we can enjoy sustained stillness with God. I used to feel a little guilty when I first established such a rhythm for myself leaving my husband to cope with the family. When we discovered that I would come back from such times rested, refreshed and more capable of coping with the stresses and strains of life, my husband actively encouraged these times alone with God!

Homework

Think: Is there a time when you could pray most days? Find out whether there are Quiet Days and retreats in your area and join in.

A prayer

Stir up in me such a desire for you that prayer becomes a priority.

Matthew 9:15 (NIV)

Fasting

This week we have been caught up in a number of paradoxes. We have observed that, like Jesus, we can pray anywhere and everywhere yet there is special value in having a prayer place. We have also seen that we can pray at any time but there is value in making and keeping appointments with God. And we have highlighted the importance of coming to God with great expectations: that he will hear, bless and reward us; that, equally, we need to come with all our antennae out, ready to receive what he longs to give.

Before we leave the subject of preparing to pray, we need to reflect on one more assumption Jesus appears to make—that our praying will be accompanied by fasting.

Jesus not only said, 'When you pray...' Almost in the same breath, he continued, 'When you fast...' Note that he did not say, 'If you fast' but 'When you fast' (Matthew 6:16) as though, in his mind, fasting and praying are two sides of the same coin. Furthermore, when John's disciples asked why his disciples did not fast Jesus replied:

How can the guests of the bridegroom mourn while he is with them? The time will come when the bridegroom will be taken from them; then they will fast.

Many Christians believe that the time Jesus refers to is now. They have discovered that one reason why fasting is valuable is that it helps to expose the things that control us.

Food so easily camouflages emotions which consume us: anger, impatience, anxiety. If we decide to deprive the body of one meal a week or of all meals one day a week, these obsessional feelings will rise to the surface and, although this can be distressing, it reveals some of the hindrances to our prayer. But fasting also sharpens our concentration so that we can use the time we would have spent preparing or eating food praising God and deepening our relationship with him.

Homework

Reflect on this claim: 'Perhaps in our affluent society fasting involves far larger sacrifice than the giving of money.'

Richard Foster, Celebration of Discipline

A prayer

Pray that you may take seriously Jesus' invitation to find a time and a place to pray, a rhythm of prayer which works for you for now, and that your praying and worshipping will be laced by fasting.

JH

Acts 1:4,5 (NIV)

The Holy Spirit's role

Between his Resurrection and his Ascension, Jesus said to his disciples:

'Do not leave Jerusalem, but wait for the gift my Father promised, which you have heard me speak about . . . In a few days you will be baptised with the Holy Spirit.'

Jesus was urging them to do nothing until they had received the Father's special gift of the Holy Spirit. Elsewhere in the New Testament, it becomes clear that the Holy Spirit has a vital role to play in teaching us to pray. But before we examine precisely how he helps us with our prayer, we need to remind ourselves who the Holy Spirit is.

Jesus describes him as the Paraclete (John 14:26), a Greek word which is variously translated the Comforter, the Advocate or the Counsellor and which means someone called to the side of another because they are qualified to help— like the doctor we call when we are sick or the solicitor we employ when we need legal advice. In using the words 'another Comforter' (John 14:26) Jesus selects a term which means 'of the same kind'. The implication is that this Comforter is just like Jesus: 'Jesus' other self.'

Like Jesus, then, the Holy Spirit is an attractive personality. Commenting on the spiritual harvest which he produces in the life of the believer, Robert Frost observes: 'Only a lovely person can minister love. Only a joyful person can minister joy. Only a peaceful person can minister peace.' This lovely, joyful, peaceful person empowers us, enabling us to do what we could not do alone, including discovering how to pray.

Homework

Reflect on an insight of William Temple's: 'It is no good giving me a play like "Hamlet" or "King Lear" and telling me to write a play like that. Shakespeare could do it: I can't. And it is no good showing me a life like the life of Jesus and telling me to live a life like that. Jesus could do it; I can't. But if the genius of Shakespeare could come and live in me, then I could write plays like that. And if the Spirit of Jesus could come and live in me, I could live a life like that.'

A prayer

Rejoice that the Spirit has come and pray:
O Comforter draw near,
Within my heart appear,
And kindle it Thy holy flame
bestowing.

Bianco da Siena, tr. R. F. Littledale

Romans 8:16; John 20:22 (NIV)

The Spirit convinces us we are loved

Yesterday we stood on the threshold of a vital discovery—that without the Holy Spirit we cannot pray. For the next six days we shall examine how the Holy Spirit helps us to pray like Jesus. The first clue comes in Paul's letter to the Romans, where he claims that it is the Holy Spirit who enables us to call God 'Abba, Father'. Furthermore,

The Spirit himself testifies with our spirit that we are God's children.

This claim could open the door to prayer for all those who protest that they cannot possibly call God 'Daddy' because of the hurts which have been inflicted on them by their earthly fathers. When such people see how close Jesus was to his Father and when it is suggested to them that, like Jesus, they come to the Father full of trust and confidence, they feel disadvantaged.

But if we take Paul's teaching seriously, the past need no longer present us with an insurmountable obstacle. The Holy Spirit can either bypass it to convince us that God is a loving parent-figure and that we are his children. Or, he can come into our bruised and battered emotions and so heal us that the veil is removed from our eyes and we recognize that, although our earthly father may have failed us for a whole variety of reasons, our heavenly Father is not like that—his love for us is unconditional and never-ending. It always enfolds us. Such a realization, when the truth of it trickles from our head into our heart, is liberating. It transforms our prayer life.

Homework

On the first Easter evening, Jesus appeared to his disciples as they gathered together in the Upper Room. There 'he breathed on them and said, "Receive the Holy Spirit"' (John 20:22). Imagine that you are there in the room with the disciples, that Jesus comes to you and says those words. Allow him to breathe his breath and energy and personality into you.

A prayer

Spirit divine, attend our prayers,
And make this house thy home:
Descend with all thy gracious powers:
O come, great Spirit come!
Come as the wind: sweep clean away
What dead within us lies,
And search and freshen all our souls
With living energies.

Johann Cruger

Ephesians 2:18 (GNB)

The Spirit gives access to the Father

Yesterday we observed that the Holy Spirit is the One who sets us free to call God Father. But Paul reminds us that he does more than that. Together with Jesus, he gives us access to the Father.

It is through Christ that all of us, Jews and Gentiles, are able to come in the one Spirit into the presence of the Father.

Commenting on this verse Francis Wale Oke writes: 'God is Spirit. We cannot contact Him through our intellect, our mind or our body. We can only contact God through our spirit. It is the Spirit of God that helps our spirit to have direct contact with God.' (*Alone With God*)

Rublev's famous icon of the Holy Trinity, or The Circle of Love as it is sometimes called, helps me to understand this. Andrei Rublev, the fifteenth-century iconographer, painted this picture to help Christians to grasp this mystery and be drawn into the love which flows so freely between the Father, the Son and the Holy Spirit. The picture is made up of three angels sitting in a circle. The angel on the right represents the Holy Spirit, the angel on the left represents the Heavenly Father and in the centre of the circle sits the Son. The movement of the heads makes it clear that, if the person of prayer wants to move into this circle, they must do so through the person on the right, the Holy Spirit. His head is inclined towards the Son whose head, in turn, leans towards the Father. Pictorially, Andrei Rublev is saying just what Paul said—if we want to find the way to the Father, we come through Jesus by his Spirit. In turn, this reminds us that a rich and relevant prayer life exists only with the help and inspiration of the Holy Spirit.

Homework

Meditate on Jesus' claim: 'God is Spirit, and only by the power of his Spirit can people worship him as he really is' (John 4:24 GNB).

A prayer

Lord Christ... Without your Holy Spirit who lives in our hearts, what would we be? You open for us a way towards faith, towards trust in God... Spirit of the Risen Christ, Spirit of compassion, Spirit of praise, your love for each one of us will never go away.

Brother Roger of Taizé

Ephesians 1:17 (GNB)

The Holy Spirit reveals Jesus to us

The icon I described yesterday, the icon of the Holy Trinity, is best viewed through a circle—a ring formed with the index finger and the thumb or a real ring. This highlights the circle in which the three angels sit and emphasises that, if we want to come to Jesus, we come via the Holy Spirit. Pictorially the icon is portraying a vital theological truth which Paul sums up succinctly when he prays that God would give the Christians in Ephesus:

the Spirit, who will make you wise and reveal God to you, so that you will know him.

Jesus also makes it clear that, among other things, the Holy Spirit's mission is to make God known to the believer. He does this in a whole variety of ways. One is through our intellect, by reminding us of all that Jesus said and did (John 14:26), by confirming that Jesus really is who he claimed to be (John 15:26), by bringing glory to the Son and by interpreting Jesus' mind and teaching (John 16:14). Another is through our emotions by leading us into 'complete truth' (John 16:7,13).

Commenting on the phrase, 'the complete truth', Henri Nouwen explains that this phrase is closely related to the word 'betrothal'; it means that the Holy Spirit will lead us into full intimacy with God. All effective prayer stems from a love-relationship with God, we are utterly dependent on the Holy Spirit for an effective prayer life. As Paul says, we cannot even call Jesus 'Lord' without the Holy Spirit's enabling.

Homework

Respond to this challenge: 'To be filled with the Spirit . . . is not an option; it is a necessity, it is God's command: "be filled with the Spirit" (Ephesians 5:18).'

Francis Wale Oke, *Alone With God*

A prayer

Father, I pray that out of the wealth of your glory you will strengthen my inner being with your Spirit, So that Christ will make his home in my heart and so that I may have my roots in love and make love the foundation of my entire existence. Reveal to me just how broad and long, how high and deep the love of Christ is, so that I may be filled to overflowing with the very nature of Christ.

An adaptation of Ephesians 3:14–21 (GNB)

Romans 8:26,27 (GNB)

The Holy Spirit helps us in our weakness

'Pray then like this—Our heavenly Father' (Matthew 6:9 JB). said Jesus. His indwelling Spirit enables us to cry out from deep within us 'Abba! Daddy' (Galatians 4:6), to enjoy intimacy with the heavenly Father. Paul also reminds us that the Holy Spirit helps us in other ways:

The Spirit himself pleads with God for us in groans that words cannot express. And God, who sees into our hearts, knows what the thought of the Spirit is; because the Spirit pleads with God on behalf of his people and in accordance with his will.

In other words, the Spirit himself prays in us and through us, with us and for us, making us vehicles of his own prayer. He does not necessarily use words when he prays. Often he uses inarticulate groans and even tears. That is why, when he burdens us to pray for someone in trouble or for a national or international crisis, we will not find words with which to pray. Instead, we might find ourselves weeping, aching inside or groaning or sighing in prayer. We must learn to recognize that this kind of wordless prayer is just as effective as using a language we can understand.

Because it is the Spirit praying in us and through us, and because the Father reads the mind of the Spirit, we can be confident that this non-verbal prayer is heard and understood by the One to whom it is addressed: the Father. Even prayers which seem like little more than a yearning are signs that the Spirit is praying in us. As Maria Boulding puts it in *The Coming of God*: 'All your love, your stretching out, your hope, your thirst, God is creating in you so that he may fill you. It is not your desire that makes it happen, but his. He longs through your heart . . . he is on the inside of the longing.'

Homework
Ask yourself what kind of help you need with your prayer. Then ask God's Spirit to help you with that need.

A reflection
Prayer is the soul's sincere desire,
Uttered or unexpressed,
The motion of a hidden fire
That trembles in the breast.
Prayer is the burden of a sigh,
The falling of a tear,
The upward glancing of an eye,
When none but God is near.

James Montgomery

125

Romans 8:26,27 (GNB)

The Holy Spirit helps us intercede

God has not abandoned us to learn the art form of prayer on our own. He has provided us with a Teacher-Helper: his Holy Spirit. This Holy Spirit lives in us so we can pray anywhere and everywhere and at any time. He knows us so he can set us free to be real in the way I described in the first week of this School of Prayer. And, because he is so close to Christ, he discerns the prayer the Great Intercessor is expressing in any situation. As Paul puts it:

The Spirit comes also to help us, weak as we are. For we do not know how we ought to pray; the Spirit himself pleads with God for us in groans that words cannot express. And God, who sees into our hearts, knows what the thought of the Spirit is; because the Spirit pleads with God on behalf of his people and in accordance with his will.

This comes as a great relief to a whole variety of Christians who readily admit that there are occasions when they simply don't know how to pray—such as when someone is sick. Should we pray for healing, knowing that God delights to perform miracles, or should we pray that the person should be given the strength to endure pain, knowing that pain is sometimes the megaphone through which God speaks to a deaf world? The secret is to discover how Jesus is praying for that person. Jesus is alive and always interceding for us (Hebrews 7:25). It is therefore our responsibility to discover how he is praying in any given situation and to bring our prayer in line with his. If we are praying contrary to the prayer of Jesus we are wasting our breath. The person who can reveal to us the heart and mind and will of Jesus is the Holy Spirit: Jesus' other self.

Homework
Think of a person or situation about which you are praying. Ask the Holy Spirit to show you what Jesus is praying for in this situation and join in with his prayer.

A prayer
Day by day, O dear Lord, three things I pray
To see Thee more clearly,
Love Thee more dearly,
Follow Thee more nearly, day by day.
Based on Richard of Chichester's prayer

Galatians 5:22 (GNB)

The Holy Spirit changes us

The Holy Spirit is sometimes likened to water. I was thinking about this imagery as I was sitting on a shingle beach recently. As I sat at the water's edge playing with the tiny multi-coloured stones at my feet, I noticed that, while the dry stones seemed comparatively dull, those washed by the waves lapping the shore shone like jewels and revealed the splendour of their full colours: the greens and browns, blacks and pinks, creams and golds. Just as water changes dull stones into sparkling gems, so the Holy Spirit changes us. As Paul puts it:

The Spirit produces love, joy, peace, patience, kindness, goodness, faithfulness, humility, and self-control.

The love Paul describes means unselfish affection and unceasing activity which benefits the loved one. Joy means the ability to rejoice in spite of difficult places and difficult people. The peace he mentions keeps us serene in the middle of trials. Longsuffering is that quality which helps us to be patient with others, faithfulness includes a reliability and dependability which never disappoint others or let them down. Self-control involves living a balanced, disciplined life which is in perfect working order.

This harvest of the Spirit cannot be produced in our own strength. It can be reaped by the Spirit, however. Indeed, this fruit must gradually mature in the life of anyone who claims to be a person of prayer because, as Thomas Merton loved to remind us, 'To pray is to change.' Prayer must be seen as a way in which we are changed into the likeness of Christ and the place where our minds and desires are brought into alignment with his.

Homework

Look back over the Prayer School notes, revising the suggestions Jesus made: that we should find a time and a place to pray, that we should come to prayer with high expectations and alertness and recall what has been written about the role the Holy Spirit plays in the life of prayer. Recognize where you most need help and ask God to send his Spirit to help you.

A prayer

Lord, I know not what I ought to ask of you. You only know what I need. You know me better than I know myself... Teach me to pray. Pray yourself in me.

Archbishop Francois Fenelon

JH

John 8:32 (RSV)

Reality

And you will know the truth, and the truth will make you free.

A few years ago I travelled up to London for an evening discussion. It was a very hot summer night, and the upstairs meeting room was packed solid.

Sitting on the floor with my knees jammed under my chin, hot and uncomfortable, I was thanking God that the meeting was drawing to a close, when I suddenly realized that the man sitting three feet away from me on a chair was a very well known Christian speaker and Bible scholar. He was the sort of man whose reputation for spiritual insight sometimes causes people to gabble hysterically about how well their walk with the Lord is going, or emit shrill cries of 'Hallelujah!' and 'Praise the Lord!' to indicate soundness. How awful it would be, I thought, if he 'saw' something I did in 1972, just by looking into my face. Just then he took a piece of paper from his pocket and began to write something on it. He then folded the paper and, to my abject horror, leaned over and handed it to me. I unfolded it with trembling fingers and was about to read it when—the lights when out!

Sitting in the darkness, holding my piece of paper with 1972 scrawled over it for all I knew, I just wanted to die. When power was restored I saw that the man had written: 'Can you give me a few moments afterwards?' A few minutes later I followed him down the stairs like a little doggy to a small room, where he further alarmed me by announcing that he was in the habit of having visions, and that one of his recent visions involved me. It had nothing (I was thankful to hear) to do with 1972—not that I *did* anything in 1972, I hasten to add. Oh, the relief!

As we stood up to leave I couldn't help wondering if he'd read my books. He must have known what I was thinking. 'I've read your books,' he said, 'and I'd like you to know that the verse that's usually translated "The truth will make you free", can also be translated "*Reality* will make you free".'

It was a confirmation and an assurance, and it has been at the centre of everything I've thought, written and spoken about since that day.

A question
Can I handle reality?

John 3:1–3 (RSV)

The funny bike

Now there was a man of the Pharisees, named Nicodemus, a ruler of the Jews. This man came to Jesus by night and said to him, 'Rabbi, we know that you are a teacher come from God; for no one can do these signs that you do, unless God is with him.' Jesus answered him, 'Truly, truly, I say to you, unless one is born anew, he cannot see the kingdom of God.'

The reality of what we refer to casually as 'The Christian life' is quite different from the reality of life outside the Kingdom of God. I hope that doesn't sound too airy-fairy or abstract, because the spiritual life is, in fact, more practical and gritty than any other. Read again about the carpenter who got involved in mass-catering and ended up nailed to a piece of wood, if you don't believe me. Jesus was telling Nicodemus that the whole axis of his life needed to change if he wanted to enter the Kingdom. Being born again means a new context, a new perspective, new priorities and new behaviours.

The other day my wife and I went to a summer fair at the junior school where our five-year-old Katy is a pupil. One of the outdoor attractions was a bicycle that steers the wrong way. You've probably seen them—most annoying contraptions. When you turn the handlebars to the left the front wheel turns to the right, and vice-versa. The owners of this awkward vehicle were offering a prize of one pound to anyone who could ride the bicycle for six yards without putting a foot on the ground. It cost twenty pence for each attempt, and they were making lots of money because not a single person was able to adjust mentally and physically to this change in cause and effect. It was very funny to watch them trying.

Following Jesus involves a rather similar revolution in our steering habits, and many people fall by the wayside because of poor teaching in this area. 'Love your enemies.' How about that one? The world steers to the right, but we are called to do the opposite. My heart fails me sometimes when I look at the commitment that's required, but I want to live in the Kingdom of God, so I shall go on practising, however many times I fall off.

Prayer
Teach me to steer, Lord.

Matthew 16:21–24 (RSV)

Straight talking

From that time Jesus began to show his disciples that he must go to Jerusalem and suffer many things from the elders and chief priests and scribes, and be killed, and on the third day be raised. And Peter took him and began to rebuke him saying, 'God forbid, Lord! This shall never happen to you.' But he turned and said to Peter, 'Get behind me, Satan! You are a hindrance to me; for you not on the side of God, but of men.' Then Jesus told his disciples, 'If any man would come after me, let him deny himself and take up his cross and follow me...'

There is a dearth of healthy confrontation in the church nowadays. Here we see Jesus reacting with explosive anger to Peter's inappropriate and obstructive heroics. Immense, eternal issues were under discussion, and there was Peter trying to lob a very worldly spanner into the cosmic machinery. The cross was a price that Jesus was willing to pay so that men and women could inherit eternal life, and he had no intention of being distracted by sentimental assertions.

I used to feel that Peter was rather unfairly battered by Jesus on this occasion, but when I think about my own dealings with people I'm not so sure. I was infected, very early in my Christian life, with the politeness disease. Everything I said had to be expressed 'nicely', and if I did have anything negative to say it had to be done 'in love', which meant that I had approached the point in such a circumlocutory way that the recipient of my wonderful wisdom found it very difficult to know what I was talking about. I'm all for courtesy and love, but I think I have often used them as excuses for not being direct when it's necessary.

It's a matter of reality again. For a long time I saw one particular man every week for two or three hours. After months of nervously skirting around the issue I finally told him what I thought about his situation. 'Why didn't you say that before?' he asked. Exactly.

A question

How can we develop a proper assertiveness?

Daniel 1:11–16 (RSV)

Standing firm

Then Daniel said to the steward whom the chief of the eunuchs had appointed over Daniel, Hananiah, Mishael and Azariah; 'Test your servants for ten days; let us be given vegetables to eat and water to drink. Then let our appearance and the appearance of the youths who eat the king's rich food be observed by you, and according to what you see deal with your servants.' So he harkened to them in this matter, and tested them for ten days. At the end of ten days it was seen that they were better in appearance and fatter in flesh than all the youths who ate the king's rich food. So the steward took away their rich food and the wine they were to drink, and gave them vegetables.

Here's a chap who understood the 'funny bike' principle. As far as we know, Daniel never once compromised his religious principles, no matter which Babylonian king he happened to be dealing with at the time. This was his first challenge, and he came through it with flying colours. After ten days he and his companions were fitter and stronger than those who had eaten the rich court food. What a fortune he would have made nowadays. Daniel the Israelite's low-fat, vegetable only, hip 'n thigh diet would have hit the best-seller list within a fortnight. Daniel's only interest was in doing the will of his God, his reward the discovery that he would receive divine support if he stood up for what he believed in.

This unwavering attitude of Daniel's makes us feel quite threatened.

I'd like to be him *after* his brave stance was endorsed by God, but I suspect that when faced with the original dilemma I would have said in sensible, no-nonsense tones: 'Look, I honestly think that fanaticism is a poor witness. I reckon it takes more courage to eat the king's food—I honestly do…' For Daniel, though, it was the thin end of the wedge. From now on it could only get easier to do the right thing and make the right decisions. By the time he arrived (as an old man) at the famous lion sketch he must have had a profound understanding of the principle that our most crucial needs are met and satisfied by doing what we are told.

A prayer
Lord, I am not brave,
but I want to be.

Matthew 18:2,3 (RSV)

The eyes of a child

And calling to him a child, he put him in the midst of them, and said, 'Truly, I say to you, unless you turn and become like children you will never enter the kingdom of heaven.'

Jesus seems to be saying here that the reality of heavenly things is more apparent to childlike eyes than to the eyes of sophistication and 'grown-upness'.

A couple of years ago we took our bicycles down to Newhaven, crossed on the ferry to Northern France, and spent a few very enjoyable days pedalling from town to town along the river valleys. Our last day was set aside to explore the port of Dieppe before recrossing the Channel that evening.

Just after lunch we entered the cool interior of a big church near the centre of town. I lost touch with the others for a while, but after a few minutes I discovered Katy, aged four, staring silently at a life-size sculpture of Mary, the mother of Jesus, holding her son's dead body in her arms, and looking into his face with an expression of real pain and loss. Katy turned and saw me.

'Daddy,' she asked, 'why has Jesus got a hole in his side?' Stumblingly, I explained that a Roman spear had been responsible. Katy was horrified. She studied the sculp-

ture again. 'Daddy, he's got holes in his feet. Why's he got holes in his feet?'

'Look.' I pointed to a small crucifix on the wall above us. 'They nailed his feet to that piece of wood called a cross, and those are the holes where the nails were.' 'Nailed his feet?!' She turned to look at the stone figures again. Her voice broke a little as she spoke. 'Daddy, he's got holes in his hands as well. They didn't nail his hands as well, did they?' Sadly, I explained. Katy moved closer to the sculpture, put her arm around Jesus and rested her face down on his knee.

Suddenly I longed to go back to the time when I first understood that Jesus died for me and it really hurt, before I covered my faith in words and worries. I wanted to be like a child again.

A prayer

Father, give me the eyes of a child.

John 3:16 (RSV)

What is your name?

For God so loved the world that he gave his only Son, that whoever believes in him should not perish but have eternal life.

I've had a love/hate relationship with this verse since I was converted (whatever that means) at the age of sixteen. It expresses, of course, the greatest reality of all, but back in the sixties it seemed to be used almost as a talisman by the young evangelicals who thought that the Bible might be the fourth person of the Trinity. I swallowed my hate for John 3:16 years ago. Now I love it, because it encapsulates the great truth that God is crackers about us. It ought to make us feel glad and proud (in the best sense) but an awful lot of Christians feel neither of those things. Many of us have a very poor self-image, a phenomenon that has little or nothing to do with pride and humility.

I remember a woman I met when I was signing books after a meeting one evening at some church in the north of England. She held a book out for me to sign and I asked, as I always do, for her name, so that I could write a dedication to her on the title page.

'Oh,' she said, shaking her head uncertainly, 'I'm not anybody really. Just sign it…'

'Go on, tell me your name,' I coaxed. 'You must be somebody.'

She blushed slightly.

'Oh, well, I'm just Sarah…'

God so loved just Sarah that he gave his only beloved son, that if just Sarah believes in him, she will not perish but have everlasting life. Why doesn't she believe that? There could be all sorts of reasons, but perhaps one might be that the church puts far less value on Sarah than God does. The last couple of decades have seen an increased emphasis on individual spiritual achievement in certain areas. Getting and gaining from God in all sorts of quick-fix ways has tended to obscure and replace the kind of long-term care and valuing of individuals that should characterize the body of Christ. God loved the person who sits beside me in church enough to send Jesus. There aren't any nonentities.

A prayer
Father, teach us to value each other and ourselves. Thank you for sending Jesus just for me.

Luke 1:26–30 (GNB)

Blessings and troubles

In the sixth month of Elizabeth's pregnancy God sent the angel Gabriel to a town in Galilee named Nazareth. He had a message for a girl promised in marriage to a man named Joseph, who was a descendant of King David. The girl's name was Mary. The angel came to her and said, 'Peace be with you! The Lord is with you and has greatly blessed you!'

Mary was deeply troubled by the angel's message, and she wondered what his words meant. The angel said to her, 'Don't be afraid, Mary; God has been gracious to you . . .'

Mary is one of my all-time heroes, or heroines, or heroic persons, and this particular passage contains a clue to the reason why I hold her in such high regard. She was a realist, a good servant, and a very puzzled lady. Mary is told by the angel that she is 'greatly blessed'. She is immediately 'deeply troubled'. For the rest of her life Mary continues to be greatly blessed and deeply troubled as she observes the development of her extraordinary son's ministry, his appalling death and subsequent resurrection.

Mary's example should have a freeing effect on folk like myself who have somehow got the idea that the 'greatly blessed' mode is the only legitimate one. Nearly all of the Christians that I know well have passed through, are passing through, and certainly will pass through periods of being deeply troubled. How could it be otherwise? This is a wild, fallen world, and we are weak, vulnerable people with widely differing backgrounds and personalities, but sharing the same hope as Mary, that we have life and ultimate healing in Jesus.

How important it is that we accept this reality in each other without offering inappropriate ministry or implicit condemnation. Share blessings, share troubles, and, above all, share Jesus. We'll get by.

A prayer

Father, help us to look after each other without unreal expectations or unhelpful responses. Thank you for Mary who was obedient and genuine.

AP

Luke 24:13–17 (RSV)

Back to basics

That very day two of them were going to a village named Emmaus, about seven miles from Jerusalem, and talking with each other about all these things that had happened. While they were talking and discussing together, Jesus himself drew near and went with them. But their eyes were kept from recognizing him. And he said to them, 'What is this conversation which you are holding with each other as you walk?'

A rich mix of troubles and blessings is one thing, but a long desert-like experience of spiritual loneliness is quite another. As I travel around the country I am quite often faced with the fact that some folk have felt neglected by God for a very long time. I know a free-church minister in the north-east, for example, who simply cannot understand why there has been little or no spiritual development in the church that he leads. He's a talented, caring man who seems to have done all the right things, but, like the two fellows in this passage, he has ended up 'standing still, looking sad' because Jesus seems to have disappeared and the future is pointless. This man (and many others like him) are yearning to feel their hearts burn within them again, so that they too can tell others, with the deep wild excitement they once knew, that 'The Lord is risen indeed!'

There are no universal solutions to the problem of spiritual depression (I once bought a 'universal' roof-rack that fitted every model of car in the cosmos except the one that we had) but the experience of these two travellers is interesting. First, they received a metaphorical clip round the ear for being silly, but it didn't put them off—Jesus gets that sort of thing right. Then they were taken back to first principles via the Scriptures. Finally they received blessed bread from the stranger who turned out to be Jesus. *Then* their hearts burned!

It's worth a try. No-holds-barred repentance, followed by a quiet turn to Bible-basics, leading to warm and intimate communion with the person who was with us all the time, even when we were standing still and looking sad.

A prayer
We want to burn with life, Lord. Meet us, teach us and eat with us, please.

Luke 21:34–36 (RSV)

Burglars

'But take heed to yourselves lest your hearts be weighed down with dissipation and drunkenness and cares of this life, and that day come upon you suddenly like a snare; for it will come upon all who dwell upon the face of the whole earth. But watch at all times, praying that you may have strength to escape all these things that will take place, and to stand before the Son of man.'

The Bible is a strange book. There's always a bit you never noticed, usually right in the middle of a very familiar passage. Take this extract from Luke, for instance. When I tell people that Jesus mentioned three areas of worldly distraction that weigh the heart down, and that these include drunkenness, they usually look very surprised and demand to know exactly where the quote appears. The situation is not helped by the fact that I almost invariably forget the chapter and verse and have to leaf feverishly through the New Testament searching for evidence.

Dissipation, drunkenness and cares of this life. In my time I've had a paddle in the first, got out of my depth in the second, but jolly nearly drowned in the third. Some of us who are in the 'standing still, looking sad' bracket may have to face the reality that we are hanging on to concerns and preoccupations so ponderous that they cast a perpetual shadow of gloom over all other aspects of life. The habit of *worry* can be a crippling one.

No burglars came again last night
Just as they failed to come the night before
And for as many nights as I remember
No burglars yet again
Although I listened, as I always do, for them.
They did not come
They were not here again last night
And what if they should never come?
A waste of nights—I might have slept
But if I had, I feel quite sure
They would have come—those burglars,
Yes, they would have come.

A prayer

Lord, our worries cling to us like poultices. Sometimes we pray about them and they seem to go away for a while. Then they come back and we are close to despair. Help us, Lord, we don't want to be distracted from you.

Luke 15:11 (RSV)

The failed father?

And he said, 'There was a man who had two sons...'

If the story of the prodigal son had been told for the first time in this age, it would undoubtedly have been called 'The parable of the failed father'. After all, neither of his sons turned out very well, did they? One left home and spent all his money on riotous living and harlots, while the other grew up to be a sulky, po-faced individual who had no idea how to enjoy life. Something wrong with the parenting there, wouldn't you say?

Of course, Jesus was making a different point altogether and views on individual responsibility were very different at that time, and in that society. However, if we really are trying to deal with reality, let's face the fact that very many people outside the church, and not a few inside, have a big problem with this 'other view' of God's dealings with men and women. It's an old question, but here it comes again: If the creator really is omniscient and omnipotent, why did he produce creatures who were going to fail and rebel and experience suffering and pain as a result? Why doesn't he take responsibility for his own poor handiwork and planning? Doesn't he owe us a slice of heaven?

My evangelical training pops up answers to these questions with Pavlovian ease: God didn't want robots so he gave us free will. He is the potter and we are the clay, so we have no right to object. Our finite minds are incapable of comprehending his infinite and eternal purposes.

These arguments may or may not have virtue, but I can only say that they've never satisfactorily solved the problem for me. I wouldn't be a Christian now if my faith depended on an acceptance of the logic of creation and the fall. It doesn't depend on that—it depends on Jesus. Right at the centre of my chaotic, shifting, strangely-shaped religious belief lies the person of Jesus and the relationship that exists between us. He is the still point from which all references are taken and I have gradually learned that he is reliable.

I can't solve the problem of the 'failed' father, but Jesus knows the truth and I trust him. In the end—that is my answer.

A prayer
Father, there are lots of things I don't understand. Help me not to pretend I do when I don't. Thank you again for Jesus.

Matthew 14:6–12 (RSV)

Time out

But when Herod's birthday came, the daughter of Herodias danced before the company, and pleased Herod, so that he promised with an oath to give her whatever she might ask. Prompted by her mother, she said, 'Give me the head of John the Baptist here on a platter.' And the king was sorry; but because of his oaths and his guests he commanded it to be given; he sent and had John beheaded in the prison and his head was brought on a platter and given to the girl, and she brought it to her mother. And his disciples came and took the body and buried it; and they went and told Jesus.

There was a time when even Jesus became still and sad. He was a real man, so it isn't surprising. Jesus and his cousin must have been very close. Their parents knew each other, they were the same age, and they lived within a day's journey of each other. Even before they were born John had leaped in his mother's womb when the excited Mary hurried to Elizabeth's hill-country home to describe her encounter with an angel. I may be wrong, but I've always felt that Jesus' impassioned outburst about John in the seventh chapter of Luke's Gospel contains a very personal note as well as a logical argument.

Now, on hearing that John is dead, he tries to find a place to be alone, a place to grieve, but the crowds are like baby birds, knowing only their own hunger, and as he sets foot on the shore they all are waiting for him. Business as usual. No more time for grief.

A prayer
Thank you, Father, for this special view of one of your son's very personal moments. I'm sorry he was made so sad by his cousin's death, and I want to thank you that he got on with the job so determinedly after drawing apart for a while. It gives me permission to do the same.

Zephaniah 3:15–20 (RSV)

God of the gaps

Do not fear, O Zion; let not your hands grow weak. The Lord, your God, is in your midst, a warrior who gives victory; he will rejoice over you with gladness, he will renew you in his love; he will exult over you with loud singing as on a day of festival. 'I will remove disaster from you, so that you will not bear reproach for it. Behold, at that time I will deal with all your oppressors. And I will save the lame and gather the outcast, and I will change their shame into praise and renown in all the earth. At that time I will bring you home, at that time when I gather you together; yea, I will make you renowned and praised among all the peoples of the earth, when I restore your fortunes before your eyes,' says the Lord.

This passage, and the last sentence in particular, became very important to me six or seven years ago when I retreated from my normal responsibilities and activities because of a stress-related illness. One thing that assisted my recovery was the daily discipline of writing, a completely new occupation for me. There was something very therapeutic about taking feelings and memories from inside and placing them outside, on a sheet of paper. Gradually, the notion of becoming a full-time writer began to form in my mind. My family were very supportive, but most other people displayed a thinly-veiled scepticism when I described what I intended. I can hardly blame them. I had a mortgage, three children and a dog to support. How was I going to provide for them? Then, one morning, I read the final part of Zephaniah, and those last few words stood out like divine braille, penetrating the spiritual blindness that I was suffering at the time. God was going to restore my fortunes before my eyes, and although it was difficult to picture how it would happen, I felt sure that writing would be involved somehow. Soon after that I sent a selection of written pieces to the American writer, Elizabeth Sherrill, who, with her husband John, had been responsible for a string of best-selling books, including *The Cross and the Switchblade*. Elizabeth replied with the kind of letter raw beginners dream of. Armed with her generous encouragement I continued to wear out biros and tear up rejection slips from publishers informing that 'our readers would not approve of our Lord Jesus Christ being written about in that fashion...'

But God kept his promise.

A question
Are we too quick to plug 'gaps'?

139

1 Corinthians 13:8–10 (RSV)

Long live love

Love never ends; as for prophecies, they will pass away; as for tongues, they will cease; as for knowledge, it will pass away. For our knowledge is imperfect and our prophecy is imperfect; but when the perfect comes, the imperfect will pass away.

Most people are fond of this passage, but there is nothing sentimental about what Paul is saying. All of the spiritual gifts will pass away, but love will remain. We are not saved by tongues, prophecy, words of knowledge, or any of the other useful pots and pans that equip the Christian kitchen. God is love and we are saved by the power of love. The other things are good but imperfect.

I have a friend who is a Jewish rabbi in the reformed movement. We are always looking for common ground. He is a very spiritual man and I am an Anglican. When David came to tea with his wife recently I put the following scenario to him.

'I arrive in heaven, right?' David nodded. 'And God says to me, "I'm awfully sorry, Adrian, but Jesus *wasn't* the Son of God. The Jews got it right and you didn't. But will you trust me anyway?"'

'Yes,' smiled David, 'I can imagine that quite easily.'

'Hold on,' I said, 'I haven't finished yet. While I'm chewing over what God's said to me—you roll up.'

'Oh,' said the rabbi, his smile fading a little.

'"Hello, David," says God, "I'm awfully sorry, but Jesus *was* the Son of God. You missed out on the Messiah. But will you trust me anyway?"'

'And what happens then?' asked David.

'Well, I guess you and I talk it over just outside heaven's gate, then we go to God arm in arm and say that as long as the three of us can be together nothing else matters.'

'Hmmm,' said David thoughtfully.

Don't throw scriptural thunderbolts at me. I *do* believe that Jesus is exactly who and what he said he was, but I also believe that the love between David and me is as real and as lasting as anything else.

Reflect
John Lennon was right. 'Love is real . . .'

John 16:4b–7 (GNB)

The helper

I did not tell you these things at the beginning, for I was with you. But now I am going to him who sent me, yet none of you asks me where I am going. And now that I have told you, your hearts are full of sadness. But I am telling you the truth: it is better for you that I go away, because if I do not go, the Helper will not come to you. But if I do go away, then I will send him to you.

It was an astonishing thing for Jesus to say—and the disciples (not for the first time) were slow to understand. 'It is better for you that I go away.' How could it be? They loved him and needed him. They had followed him since the start of his ministry, and for three years he had taught them and told them about God the Father as no one had ever done before. But then no one ever could have done—because this was God the Son, unique in all the world. Imagine what it was like for them to live in the presence of the Son of God, and learn from him, and spend all their days with him, and eat all their meals with him.

'Better for you that I go away...' How could it be? It was his presence that was so wonderful—and that's what they wanted, not his absence. And it was his presence they were going to have, in a way that was even more wonderful than the last three years had been. Then his physical presence was there for them—if they were there with him. But if they weren't there then they couldn't enjoy his presence and they couldn't go on discovering about

God from his teaching. And if they needed his help they couldn't have it—if he wasn't there. But in the future they *would* have his help, and his presence. Not his physical presence, but his spiritual presence. And not outside them, but inside them.

The Spirit of Jesus would come and live in their hearts—and in all our hearts right down to the present day, if we will receive him. When you go to Holy Communion, and eat the bread that is the body of Christ, and drink the wine that is the blood of Christ, realize afresh that Christ is in you—God with us—Emmanuel. Not outside you. Inside you—like the bread and the wine. God the Holy Spirit. The Counsellor, the Comforter and the Helper. There for you—and, through you, for the world that he made and loves and longs for.

So be deeply thankful—and admit that what Jesus said to his disciples was true—for them and for us. 'I am telling you the truth: it is better for you that I go away, because if I do not go the Helper will not come to you.'

SB

Micah 4:6,7 (RSV)

Coming last

In that day, says the Lord, I will assemble the lame and gather those who have been driven away and those whom I have afflicted; and the lame I will make the remnant; and those who were cast off, a strong nation; and the Lord will reign over them in Mount Zion from this time forth and for evermore.

A friend and I took some members of the local youth club to Wales a few years ago. I was a little nervous because I knew that the weekend itinerary included the climbing of a very high mountain, and I seriously doubted that I was fit enough to manage it. No rock-climbing was involved, just walking and clambering forever. I was sure my lungs and legs would rebel long before I reached the top.

Because of this apprehension I set off like an express train when we started, anxious to put failure or success behind me as quickly as possible. Some of the kids kept pace with my frenetic attack on the hillside, while others; the plump, the wrongly-shod, the frail and the disinclined dribbled slowly along at the rear. It wasn't until I was about three-quarters of the way to the top and I stopped to admire the view (I claimed) that I took any notice of what was happening to the stragglers. Far, far below me, I could see a little line of bent figures toiling laboriously up the slope, and, right at the back, my friend and co-leader, Michael, who was much fitter than me and could easily have been further on than I was by now. As I watched, he stopped to encourage the smaller figure in front of him who seemed to have given up temporarily. I reached the top long before Michael. It took him hours to shepherd his reluctant lambs to the summit.

Sometimes it can look as if the elevated, front-running, high profile Christians are the significant, successful ones, but it is not so. Those who are carrying out the commission implied by these verses in Micah are the winners in God's eyes, for their example and their inspiration is Jesus himself.

A prayer
Father, give us patience and pleasure in helping those who are having trouble making it.

John 10:10 (RSV)

Serious fun

The thief comes only to steal and kill and destroy; I came that they may have life, and have it abundantly.

I was speaking at a youth festival on the east coast last year. It was a very lively event and the young people seemed to be enjoying themselves.

'I think it makes it easier for them to take in the serious things when they're having fun like this.'

It was one of the organizers who made this comment as we stood together and watched a laughing, scuffling, happy queue of teenagers waiting to enter a large tent where a popular band was due to perform. I agreed at the time largely because I suffer from chronic nodding-itis. Later, when I thought about what the chap had said, I remembered all the church youth-group leaders who have expressed to me their bewilderment about conflicting behaviours by the young people they are responsible for. They couldn't understand why decent, arm-raising, praise-emitting Sunday teenagers could change into such monstrous beings on some 'secular' occasions. Actually, this is merely the nature of the beast, broadly speaking, and it's probably a healthier attitude to life than the one taken by many repressed adult church-goers. Healthy teenagers look for life, and then enter it.

What could be more serious for the youngsters at that festival than to have fun? What more could one ask than that they learn to associate guilt-less and exuberant living with the institution of the church? Perhaps we should be hoping that our young people will grow up to be like King David, who was whole-hearted in sorrow and repentance. Jesus promised us life in abundance— not emotional restraint and eternal moderation.

Consider this—God thought it worthwhile to send his son to die for us so that we could enjoy eternal life. What will this life be? I don't know the answer to that question any more than you do, but I do know that it will contain the essence of everything that is bright and strong and beautiful and satisfying and peaceful and dynamic and real.

A prayer

Father, help us to accept your gift of abundant life and avoid preventing anyone else from finding it. Thank you in advance.

New Daylight BRF © 1993

The Bible Reading Fellowship
Peter's Way, Sandy Lane West, Oxford, OX4 5HG
ISBN 0 7459 2559 6

Also in Australia
St Mark's Canberra, P O Box E67, Queen Victoria
Terrace, Canberra, ACT 2600

Distributed in the USA by
The Evangelical Education Society of the Protestant
Episcopal Church, 2300 Ninth Street South, Suite
301, Arlington, VA 22204

The Bible Reading Fellowship
P O Box M, Winter Park, Florida 32790

Publications distributed to more than 60 countries

Acknowledgments

American Bible Society (*Good News Bible*)
copyright 1966, 1971 and 1976, published by the
Bible Societies and Collins;

The Central Board of Finance of the Church of
England (material from *The Alternative Service
Book 1980*);

Darton, Longman & Todd (*New Jerusalem Bible*);

Division of Christian Education of the National
Council of the Churches of Christ in the USA (*Revised
Standard Version and New Revised Standard
Version*);

International Bible Society (*New International
Version*);

Revised English Bible © 1989 by permission of
Oxford and Cambridge University Presses;

Extracts from the Book of Common Prayer of 1662,
the rights in which are invested in the Crown in
perpetuity within the United Kingdom, are
reproduced by permission of the Crown's patentee,
Cambridge University Press.

Prayers for the Decade of Evangelism (pages 12 and
94) provided by the Anglican Consultative Council.

Line illustrations © Sr Elizabeth Ruth Obbard ODC

Cover photograph: Peter Baker/PhotoBank

Printed in Denmark

Theological advisers

The Rt Rev. Stuart Blanch
*Lord Blanch, former Archbishop of York
(Anglican)*

The Rev. Robert Murray
SJ DD
*Heythrop College, University of London
(Roman Catholic)*

The Rev. John Newton PhD
*Former Principal of Wesley College, Bristol
(Methodist)*